The Mystery Fancier

Volume 7, Number 5
September/October 1983

TABLE OF CONTENTS

MYSTERIOUSLY SPEAKING	Page 1
Bleeding the Fun out By Fred Isaac	Page 3
German Secondary Literature By Greg Goode	Page 7
The Crime Story in Sweden By K. Arne Blom	Page 16
IT'S ABOUT CRIME By Marvin Lachman	Page 26
REEL MURDERS Movie Reviews by Walter Albert	Page 31
VERDICTS Book Reviews	Page 35

The Mystery Fancier
(USPS:428-590)
is edited and published bi-monthly by
Guy M. Townsend
1711 Clifty Drive
Madison, IN 47250

SUBSCRIPTION RATES: Second-class mail, U.S. and Canada, $12.00 per year (6 issues); first-class mail, U.S. and Canada, $15.00; overseas surface mail, $12.00; overseas air mail, $18.00. Overseas subscribers please pay in international money order, check drawn on U.S. bank, or currency; no checks drawn on foreign banks, please.

Single copy price: $2.50
Second-class postage paid at Madison, Indiana
Copyright 1982 by Guy M. Townsend
All rights reserved for contributors
ISSN:0146-3160

Covers by Brad W. Foster

This hasn't been my day. I had gotten almost to the end of this column when I carelessly gave the computer an improper command which it could not comprehend and the tempermental bugger went catatonic on me. As it refused to accept any further commands--including the essential command to write the file to the disk--I had no choice but to press the reset button and wipe out the entire column. That is one of the very few drawbacks I have found to composing on the terminal--if something **does** go wrong, there's no rough draft lying around to redo it from. This has happened to me a time or two before, and I find it incredibly boring. What seems thoughtful or witty or significant when it comes forth spontaneously, seems forced and contrived when I try to rewrite it from memory. What generally happens is that I reduce what were pages into paragraphs, and what were paragraphs into sentences. There are some who would call this a blessing.

Finding myself in the luxurious (and unaccustomed) position of having enough articles on hand to do some elementary grouping, I could not, once I saw that Brad Foster had sent along a cartoon cover for this issue, resist the temptation to confound several groups in one fell swoop. Accordingly, the current issue will be the most academic to date. The poor sucker who picks it up in the bookstore on the basis of the cover will probably be dismayed to find so much bibliographical and critical material herein. And the serious scholar, who will undoubtedly find the contents of such value that he will want to keep the issue close at hand at all times, will certainly be embarrassed to be seen with his nose in what might at a glance appear to be a comic book. With my warped sense of humor, I was powerless to resist.

Two magazines and two catalogues need mentioning. I wrote what must have been pages about them before the screwup, but I haven't the heart to tackle it again. **Echoes**, Tom Johnson's magazine for fans of the pulps, has a handsome new look. It's typeset (or word-processed) in double columns and printed (in a slightly larger than digest size) on clean white paper. The address is 504 E. Morris St., Seymour, TX 76380, and the price is $2.25 for a single copy and $6.50 for three.

A must for Old Time Radio fans, even if you are not within the listening area of Chicago's WCFL, AM 1000, is Chuck Shaden's **Nostalgia Digest**. Articles, photos, program listings, and the incredibly low price of $7.00 for six issues make this the best bargain in town. Checks and money orders to The Hall Closet, Box 421 Morton Grove, IL 60053.

Waves Press & Bookshop (4040 MacArthur, Richmond, VA 23227)

publishes very nice (if remarkably pricey) limited edition books, and it is also in the used-book business (although, when the prices get into this range, good taste requires that they be referred to as "rare" rather than "used" books). Its "Catalogue Twenty: 260 Items of Fantasy/Detective Fiction" is now available.

Also available is Catalogue Six from Paulette Greene--Rare Books (140 Princeton Road, Rockville Centre, NY 11570). This 60 page catalogue lists nearly 800 "Mystery, Detective & Science-Fiction" first editions, all for sale at prices which are, for the serious collector, quite reasonable.

Remarkably perceptive as all TMFers are, you will have noticed that this issue is a bit late. There's a good reason for this, which I will go into in 7:6, which will be printed at the same time as this issue and will be mailed out within a week of 7:5. I am enclosing renewal forms in both 7:5 and 7:6, and I hope you will send in your renewal checks as soon as one or the other issue arrives. I am motivated in this hope by more than my usual simple greed. As it happens--and as I will explain more fully in 7:6--I am on the verge of spending several thousand dollars on new equipment for TMF, and I find myself several thousand dollars short of that amount. Please renew quickly and help me keep the wolf from my door.

No letters this time. There were just a few of them--let's get on the stick, out there--and I stuck them in 7:6. Ooops! I take that back. In rummaging through the debris on my disgustingly cluttered desk, just before printing out this column, I came across a letter from Bob Adey which had disappeared from sight on the very day I received it. Since the letter column for 7:6 is completed, and since I haven't a spare page in this issue, I'll run Bob's letter on the remainder of this space--which will confound future scholars to no end when they try to find it in "The Documents in the Case." Ah, well, what's life without a little adversity?

From Bob Adey, 1 Spring Close, Colwall, North Malvern, Worcestershire, WR13 6RE, ENGLAND:

The main point of this letter is to let you know that from December 1st we shall be resident at: 1 Spring Close, Colwall, Nr. Malvern, Worcestershire, WR13 6RE, ENGLAND. Phone number: Colwall 40139.

With books that, in terms of number, run into five figures, it's not going to be a fun move, but Colwall is a very pleasant country village and we think it's all going to be worthwhile--eventually.

Therefore the arrival of TMF was all the more welcome, though I haven't as yet had time to read it from cover to cover. I've been reading Joe Christopher's stuff with pleasure since the early days of TAD, so I'm confident of enjoying his piece on **The Nine Tailors**. Joe, in common with one or two others (McSherry, Nevins, and Lachman are a few examples), has the ability to make the academic entertaining. Alas, there are many who lack that flair.

One or two decent things on television over here. A further excellent series of Rumpole (with attendant paperback original), a very good PI spoof sketch in one of the Kelly Monteith comedy series, and a further showing of a classic whodunit, **Green for Danger**, with Alastair Sim (one of my favourite actors) as Cocky. Unfortunately, I had to go out during the screening, so instead I reread the book.[...] Also on TV, Agatha Christie's **Secret Adversary** and 10 episodes of Partners in Crime. Working very well indeed.

Bleeding the Fun out

Fred Isaac

This project has been, for me, a series of paradoxes and contradictions. For one thing, I am an academic librarian, and not a professor. But, having taught the mystery at the college level, I feel a part of the group. And I do believe that detection should be studied and examined, not simply devoured and passed off as undeserving "formula fiction."

When George agreed to my being on this panel something over six months ago, I though the talk would be fairly easy to prepare. After all, I had a great title. I needed to refresh myself on some of the critical material I read years ago, and read some more, but I knew pretty much what I wanted to say. It would be witty, charming, and as much fun as the title promised. As I did that rereading and started to think about the problems, however, I became at first uneasy, and then downright confused. The shape of the situation kept shifting, developing first edges and then sharp corners. Finally, my wife put the problem into perspective when she asked, "When you write about mysteries as an intellectual, what are you trying to do? And who are you writing for?" So today I want to begin to explore these vital questions and suggest some of the answers I have come to.

To begin with, I want to make some statements, give some premises for what I think. I expect that they are probably rhetorical, but I also suspect that few of us have confronted them seriously.

    1. We began reading mysteries for pleasure.
    2. We continue to read them, and they continue to provide the same pleasure for us.
    3. We write about them in order to inform or to instruct others, to show aspects of the books which interest us, perplex us, or strike us as worth exploring.

This last sentence leads us directly into the problem. There is indeed a vital issue there. It deals with the motives of the critic. The verbs Inform and Instruct are not interchangeable. They have vastly different connotations, though both refer to the imparting of information. Informing implies a desire to carry on a discussion, to develop an exchange of views between the parties. Instructing, on the other hand, posits a superior/inferior relationship. It suggests that the problem has been seen and pondered, classified, codified, and petrified for all time. Questions, quarrels, and comments are the life of information; for instruction they are at best unnecessary, at worst impositions.

Over the years, books about the mystery have taken a number of standard forms. One is purely fan-oriented; another is made up of histories, biographies, single-author and multi-author studies. All of these rest comfortably on our shelves alongside our research tools, bibliographies, and journals. While we may have more of them than other people, most of these books--from **Mortal Consequences**, through Dilys Winn's compilations, to the **Detectionary**--are accessible to most readers of mysteries.

Then there is the third form, the scholarly or academic study. This type tries to develop our comprehension of detection through analysis. What I have found, though, is that they all have several difficulties. For one thing, none of the authors has told us what the significance of the methodology is--that is, why they have chosen the scholarly or academic approach. Though many of them have interesting and useful ideas, they do not justify them by either critical overviews or by their results. Two examples will indicate the scope of their--and our--problem.

At one end of the spectrum is Robert Champigny's **What Will Have Happened**. Champigny seems to know a good deal about the mystery. The bibliography includes French and German books, both novels and commentaries, as well as English-language works. But his text does not deal with either the detective stories or their critical offspring. Rather, his intent is to make a "Philosophical Inquiry" into what he calls "ludic" and "hermeneutic" tales. The Fog Index, by my count, is about 15, but the book is far more difficult than that indicates. After reading Champigny's 150 pages, the reader may be convinced that the author has used his specialized learning and technical verbiage to prove their value, but their applicability to the mystery, and the literary merits of the genre, are questions that he appears not to have considered.

From the other end of the critical line, Robin Winks opens his **Modus Operandi** with an attempt to respond to Champigny's use of philosophical-critical jargon. "Those who try to analyze detective fiction according to the language of academic criticism sound shrill, foolish, or simply sad," he avers. But his book puzzles me more than it informs me. Subtitled as an "excursion," its Fog Index is at least as high as Champigny's. Where Champigny is scrupulous, Winks is casual. The tone seems light, but the sentences are highly complex. And there are sudden, unexpected shifts from analysis to personal anecdote. The result for me is an unintentioned admission by the writer of serious schizophrenia. Though he vocally denies it, Winks finds himself caught between his position as professor of history at Yale and his avocation as mystery expert at **The New Republic**.

There are other books on my shelf, and I assume yours, that lie somewhere between the intense rigor of Champigny and the attempted playfulness of Winks. Among others, William Ruehlmann's analysis of the private eye, LeRoy Panek's treatments of the Golden Age and spy writers, George Dove's investigation of the procedural, and John Cawelti's comparative study of popular forms have useful, important things to say. But as we read them, we find our minds wandering. Sometimes we think we are being patronized by the author, or that the argument being advanced is simplistic. At other times we find obvious errors of fact or typos that betray a lack of dedication. Or we argue with the writer about the correctness of some interpretation. These may be healthy acts in themselves, but they suggest a problem.

From my position as critic and analyst as well as reader, I welcome the efforts that have been made, from Champigny's and other's vantage points, for their insights and their attempts to raise the level of our discourse. But I contend, in part because of their failure to relate to various groups of readers, that their value is called into question as fewer and fewer people are willing or able to read the books they produce. Instead of attracting others to join in their discussion, they increase the distance between the reader and the critic. They end in a position analogous to the cry of the old-time nostrum salesman: "Of course my product is good for your ailment. It tastes bad, doesn't it?"

So my title here has direct relevance. What all of us, in our role as academic critics, are doing, in fact if not by design, is bleeding the fun from the mystery. We advance our scholarship, our role as instructors, over our love of the form and our continuing excitement as readers. We are trying to validate the mystery as literature for the people in bookstores, and simultaneously to prove its worth as a subject in our universities, thereby advancing our own status. But in justifying it to the academic community, we are pulled away from the public and into the intellectual world. Our serious lives as professionals amassing credentials and securing tenure are at odds with our happy lives as readers, fans, and armchair sleuths.

How did this happen? How did our joy turn into jargon? When did the thrill of the chase become prose necessitating the use of the Fog Index? There are two main reasons. One of them is the continued low regard usually accorded to mysteries, even by those who read them. A large part of this distaste can be traced to Edmund Wilson, whose three-part diatribe in **The New Yorker** remains the standard of snobbery. Using questionable judgment in his choice of books, at best perfunctory reading, and his own quirky writing style at its vitriolic best, he savaged the detective story as popular literature. We have spent the past forty years trying to restore the devastated genre to respectability after those unfair attacks.

On the other side is the uncertain status of mysteries in universities around the country. Purdue, for example, states explicitly that only articles with "suitable subject matter" and pedigrees will be considered at time of tenure and merit review decisions. (This, incidentally, holds true for librarians, who have faculty status, as well as classroom teachers.) This puts the onus on us to justify our work both as subject and as product to our peers and administrators. As experts in a not-quite-acceptable field, we must seem to be especially serious in our endeavors. The implication is that we should leave this non-literary mode and talk about "real" literature. Or, at least, if we must speak of mysteries, they should be those of Dickens and Balzac, not Christie and Hammett.

Then again, even if the work we produce is as good as we can make it, our colleagues are unlikely to appraise--and hopefully to praise--it at its full value. It is hard for one trained to think of Blood and Guts as treated in MacBeth to deal with Raymond Chandler or Robert B. Parker. And the department chairman who sees political fiction through Trollope's eyes will assuredly have trouble with James McClure and Sjowall and Wahloo.

So there is skepticism on both sides. Our friends in mystery are somewhat wary that we take our favorite writers so seriously. And our co-workers are at least unnerved that we remember, much less care about them all. We are trying, in our present attempts, to convert the unconverted, and perhaps the unconvertible. Even more frustrating, we are doing so by using a technical language which the reading public does not comprehend and will not make the effort to approach, and which the academic world does not fully accept in this context. The present situation is that as we become more dedicated to our quest, fewer people are listening.

I think there is a remedy for our dilemma, but it is not an easy one. I am convinced that the mystery is "real" literature, in part because of its broad appeal. I also think it worthy of in-depth study by academics and other critical minds. However, we must analyze and re-define our angle of vision. This does not mean a return to square one in our process of educating the public and our professional worlds. We assuredly do not need to repeat Earl Bargainnier's **Gentle Art of Murder** and the compendious **Bedside, Bathtub and Armchair Agatha Christie** in order to appreciate Poirot, Parker Pyne, and their creator.

Rather, we need to introduce the millions of readers of mysteries to lesser-known writers, men and women who are telling their stories in non-traditional ways. We should examine authors who have lost favor and need re-discovery, and others whose books have gone out of print but who are worth the trouble of searching out. And we should scrutinize the recent revival of the series (in particular Murder Ink, Scene of the Crime, and Perennial) and debate whether they are doing what they ought.

At the same time, our work can broaden the thus far narrow parameters of past work. We have begun to break down the genre into its many and complex components. We must continue this work and also show how each of them operates, both as single units and as parts of the whole. For example, the police in Country House stories have a role completely at odds with the Procedural and Hardboiled cops. In this vein we can lead an examination of the social impact of detection, the roles of institutions of power, and other problems that the mystery confronts.

My exhortation is also in part to get you--and myself--out of the nests we have built for ourselves. As good as **Clues, The Armchair Detective,** and **The Mystery Fancier** are as journals and the Popular Press and Mysterious Books are as publishers, they are only reaching a small group of readers. Writing for this narrow audience is an important, even a vital activity, but it is at best a labor-intensive one, and at worst narcissistic. We should try to develop and include broader markets. We should aim at major university and trade publishers, and at large circulation magazines through book reviews, articles, and our books. The result will be a growth in awareness and a broader appreciation of the mystery as a form by readers, and alternative ways to think about it by those who presently dismiss it as escapism and mindless trash.

What we can no longer do is sit alone in our corner, wringing our collective hands at the lack of respect our form receives. We have done plenty of narrow, single-author studies over the past few years. Some of them have been excellent. We should now take that sizeable body of literature and use it to enlarge our scope. (I plan, for example, a study of the Lockridge's North tales as studies in simultaneous detection; as I see it, Bill Weigand operates as an almost equal partner with Pamela North in the developing of the solutions.)

In the end, we have to use our passion for the mystery and our love of its problems. We cannot stand by and let it bleed to death. When, on that bitter cold morning, Sherlock Holmes burst into Watson's bedroom crying, "Come! The game is afoot. Not a word! Into your clothes and come!", did the good doctor hesitate? Faced with the challenges we have, can we?

German Secondary Literature

Greg Goode

INTRODUCTORY NOTE

While at the University of Cologne for a fellowship in philosophy, 1982-1983, I had the opportunity to contribute German entries to Walter Albert's upcoming **International Bibliography of Secondary Sources** (Brownstone Books, 1984). This article is an outcome of that research. I would like to thank the two Cologne professors mentioned in the article, Helmut Bonheim and Volker Neuhaus, for pointing me in the right directions and for many enjoyable hours of informative discussion. All translations are my own.

Strange as it may at first seem, the bulk of German secondary literature on the mystery-detective genre, perhaps sixty to seventy percent, is on English and American crime fiction. This is in part explained by the facts that there just **is** more English-language than German-language crime fiction and that in Germany there is perhaps more English-language crime fiction readily available in German translation than there is German crime fiction. In any case, the fact that most of the German critical material is on a literature originally written in a foreign language explains much of the character of German critical material.

A word should be said about the German taxonomy of the mystery-detective genre. Most German writers who do not use the English-language divisions, such as crime fiction, detective fiction, spy fiction, classical and hard-boiled schools, etc.; instead, they divide the genre more or less as follows. The genre as a whole belongs to the literary category of "trivial literature." This is like our "popular literature," but wider, because what counts in Germany as Literature proper is more restricted. Professor Volker Neuhaus, of the German Department at the University of Cologne, told me that, if they had been German writers, the works of Charles Dickens and Wilkie Collins would have been considered trivial literature.

The genre itself is called that of the crime story. Its subgenres include the detective story, the crime story, the criminal story, the mystery, the criminal adventure story, the **roman policier**, and the thriller. As these do not all mean what they appear to mean, they are summarized and explained below.

Trivial Literature is roughly equivalent to our

Popular Literature.
  Detective Story (seen primarily as British) corresponds to our British Detective Story (Doyle, Chesterton, etc.).
  Crime Story (seen primarily as American) corresponds to our Hard-boiled or Private Eye Story (Hammett, Chandler, etc.).
  Criminal Story (**Crime and Punishment, Raffles**) corresponds to our Crime Novel and "Cracksman" Story.
  Mystery corresponds to our "Gothic" Mystery (Ann Radcliffe).
  Criminal Adventure Story corresponds to our Spy or Espionage Story.
  Thriller corresponds to our Thriller or Suspense Thriller.

As can be seen, the detective story is seen to be primarily British, the crime story primarily American.

GENERAL CHARACTERISTICS

German secondary literature is heavy on abstract, general essays treating the genre as a whole, and light on biographical and bibliographical studies, as well as pieces on individual books, characters, and authors. This is perhaps to be expected, since German critics are writing about a foreign literature for the most part. Biographical and bibliographical material on English-language crime fiction is just not that easy to find in Germany. There are many books and essays entitled "The Detective Novel," "On Detective Literature," and so forth. Two of the most important books on the genre are entitled **The Crime Novel**. There is no German bibliography of either German or English-language crime fiction in book form. There is no book-length history of the German genre as a whole, though there is an excellent history of nineteenth-century German detective fiction and another on the British and American genre as a whole. Needless to say, there is no book-length bibliography of secondary sources. There **are** several important essay anthologies, as well as books and articles treating the genre sociologically, psychologically, and as material for instruction in schools. The genre's status as trivial literature is examined quite a bit, and attacks and apologies abound, ever more of the latter and less of the former. There are several book-length systematic and theoretical surveys and treatments of the genre and many articles in academic journals and nationwide newspapers.

The writers whose works are most often covered are Doyle, Poe, Chesterton, Gaboriau, Christie, Hammett, Chandler, and Edgar Wallace. Sherlockian criticism has not taken the direction in Germany it has in England and America, and is part of the mainstream criticism of the genre. It is significant that Ellery Queen, S.S. Van Dine, and Rex Stout are almost never discussed. I am not sure why, but it helps clarify the fact that German critics see the American contribution to the genre as having provided hard-boiled fiction. Many minority Great Detectives, such as Judge Dee, Charlie Chan, and Napoleon Bonaparte, are never mentioned. The books of James Hadley Chase, as well as those of Arthur Upfield, are quite popular, but are never written about. Raymond Chandler and Friedrich Durrenmatt are considered the best writers **qua** writers. Eric Ambler, Patricia Highsmith, and to some extent Chester Himes receive more critical attention in Germany than in England or America. German critics have come to the same conclusions as English-language critics have on the question of puzzle content vs. realism in the genre: the more of one, the less of the other. The little commentary that exists on dime novels and pulps comes from English-language secondary sources, which is perfectly understandable. Incidentally, there exists in Germany a vast, vast body of what could be called dime novels (Heftromane) which has mushroomed since at least the 1940's. With only a few exceptions, however, this huge fount has never been written about. This is probably because German dime novels carry the stigma of being the untouchables of the trivial literature category, "trash literature."

The most surprising thing about German secondary literature is that there is no fan activity. There are no fanzines or journals on the genre. As far as I could ascertain after six or seven months of searching, there are no criminous fan groups or organizations. Although in Germany crime novels out-sell any other form of novel, there are **science fiction** fan groups. So who writes all the essays and books? University professors, for the most part, joined by journalists, literary critics, editors, and free-lance writers. This explains the somewhat abstract level of the writing. Well-known German intellectuals such as man-of-letters Friedrich Schiller (1759-1805), playwright Bertolt Brecht, and philosopher Ernst Bloch have all contributed to the secondary literature. The direction of activity which exists in America and England, that of fan and reviewer activity preceding and perhaps awakening academic interest in the genre, is totally absent; and one cannot be sure whether it will work the other way around.

HISTORY AND HIGHLIGHTS

If one may be permitted to stretch a point, German secondary literature goes at least as far back as 1792, when Friedrich Schiller, himself the author of several criminous stories, wrote the foreword to the third German translation of the Pitaval collection of true crime cases, published in France beginning in 1734. In his foreword Schiller recommended the educational as well as entertainment value of such literature and attributed its popularity to a human tendency toward complicated and emotional situations.

Certainly by the early part of the nineteenth century, piecemeal crime-fiction criticism was blossoming, crime fiction itself being treated as part of the genre of sensational literature. There were several literary weeklies which consisted almost exclusively of reviews, such as the **Literary Weekly Paper** (**Literarischer Wochenblatt**, 1818-1898) or the forbiddingly titled **General Literary Weekly Report on All Commendable News, Domestic and Foreign, Including Literary Notes and Communications** (**Allgemeiner literarischer Wochenbericht ueber alle empfehlenswerte Neuigkeiten des In- und Auslandes nebst literarischer Notizen und Mitteilungen**, 1872-1887). The reviews and commentary treated the works of M.E. Braddon, Wilkie Collins, Ann Radcliffe, and Charles Reade, among others. Later in the nineteenth century there appeared full-length essays devoted just to crime novels, such as Adolf Stern's "Crime Novels and Crime Novellas" ("Kriminalromane und Kriminalnovellen"), published in a music weekly in 1864, or F. Chr. Ave-Lallemant's article "The Crime Novella" ("Die Kriminalnovelle"), published in a literary magazine in 1876.

In the early twentieth century there appeared what were probably the first German monographs on the genre: Alfred

Lichtenstein's work, **The Crime Novel: A Literary and Forensic-Medical Study with Appendix: Sherlock Holmes in the Cut Case (Der Criminalroman. Eine literarische und forensisch-medizinische Studie mit Anhang: Sherlock Holmes zum Fall Hau)** and Arthur Schimmelpfennig's **Contributions Toward the History of the Crime Novel (Beitraege zur Geschichte des Kriminalromans)**, both published in 1908. Although Lichtenstein's work preceded Schimmelpfennig's **Contributions** by several months, its only criminous content is on Holmes; most of the book is on medicine. Partly as a response, Schimmelpfennig published his **Contributions**, which is notable for being an excellent but short (sixteen pages!) capsule history of the crime fiction of several countries. In addition to these, there were early twentieth-century essays and monographs on the aesthetics of suspense, the control and subduction of trash literature, the relationship between crime fiction and criminology, Sherlock Holmes, Sherlock Holmes and Raffles, and the romance of crime fiction, all before 1920.

In the 1920's and 1930's such notables as Bertolt Brecht and Siegfried Kracauer wrote analyses of the genre. In the 1940's there were several doctoral dissertations on the crime novel, on topics such as German "robber" novels, Sherlock Holmes's successors, and the development of the crime story in British literature.

The high spot of the 1950's is undoubtedly the book which is sometimes called "The German Haycraft," Fritz Woelcken's **Literary Murder (Der literarische Mord**, 1953). This is the first and only book-length history of English and American crime fiction. Woelcken begins with Poe and devotes much time to Dickens and Doyle; he discusses the works of later writers as they fall under theme headings such as scientific thought, locked rooms, eccentric and normal detectives, realism in the genre, "democracy and detectives," transcendentalism, rationalism, justice and injustice, and so on. Woelcken devotes much more attention to Hammett and Chandler than does Haycraft, and he is familiar with much of the contemporary English-language critical material. Some of his insights are fresh even today.

The contributions of established academics began to make themselves felt in the 1960's. Articles began appearing in intellectual newspapers and literary journals, written primarily by professors of literature, literary critics, and other professionals. The most important result of this activity is the well-known Alewyn-Gerber controversy.[1] In an extremely influential, oft-cited article in 1963, Richard Alewyn defined the crime novel and the detective novel as follows: "The crime novel tells the story of a crime; the detective novel tells the story of the disclosure of a crime." Alewyn went on to argue that the detective story, according to this definition, goes back further than Poe, at least back to German literary romanticism. He made a case for E.T.A. ("Ghost") Hoffmann's **Mademoiselle de Scudery** (1819) as a detective story. It is also, by the way, a sort of locked-room story. In an article appearing in 1966, Richard Gerber took issue with all of Alewyn's points. Adopting a "come on, let's be sensible" attitude, Gerber argued that to consider **Crime and Punishment** a crime novel is pure theory. No one would walk into a bookshop asking for a crime novel and go away looking forward to reading Dostoyevski's classic. Gerber then proposed his own taxonomy, calling stories like **Crime and Punishment** "criminal fiction" and suggesting that the concept "criminal-sleuth-novels" (Verbrecherspuerhundromane) better captures what we mean when we refer to detective novels, even though the word is too cumbersome to use. Gerber also attacked the logic underlying Alewyn's statement that the detective novel is a child of romanticism and concluded that it was Poe who half-invented the detective story and Doyle who completed the task. Alewyn defended himself two years later (1968) in the prestigious newspaper **Die Zeit** with another article that later proved to be influential, and later appearances of it have been revised and expanded around the points of the controversy.

THE BOOM IN THE SEVENTIES

The 1970's brought a boom to the enterprise of crime fiction criticism in Germany. Important, useful, influential books appeared almost every year of this decade. Although there had been books on the subject before in which roots of criminous stories are sought in German romantic literature (such as Woelcken's, and a scholarly study by Professor Rainer Schoenhaar, **Novelle and the Criminal Schema (Novelle und Kriminalschema** [1969]), the burst of books in the seventies was rich and fruitful.

Pride of place for this decade, and perhaps for any other decade to this day, must go to Hans-Otto Huegler's utterly magnificent study of nineteenth-century German detective fiction, **Examining Magistrates, Thieftakers, Detectives: Theory and History of the German Detective Story in the 19th Century (Untersuchungsrichter-Diebsfanger-Detektive. Theorie und Geschichte der deutschen Detektiverzaehlung im 19. Jahrhundert,** 1978). This was the published version of Huegel's 1977 doctoral dissertation. What is so important about this work is that it explodes the widespread misconception, put forth by German, English, and American critics alike, that Germany has no distinctly German detective-story tradition. In doing his research Huegel "went where no man had gone before," digging in archives, libraries, second-hand bookshops, garages, attics, and flea markets and coming up with hundreds and hundreds of detective novels and stories in nineteenth-century periodicals that no critic had known existed. Huegel is able to show how the German detective story grew from late-eighteenth and early-nineteenth century sensational literature. In addition to its historical importance and ground-breaking conclusions, **Examining Magistrates** provides an original definition and theory of the detective story **per se** and has what may be the best bibliography of German secondary sources yet in print.

Perhaps second place in the decade should go to the interesting **Reclam's Guide to Crime Novels (Reclams Kriminalromanfuehrer,** 1978), compiled by two professors of German literature at McGill University. Part of publisher Reclam's series of guides on topics in the arts and on cultural subjects, the **Guide to Crime Novels** is a chunky, 455-page potpourri of historical information, encyclopedia entries, and survey essays on the crime novel around the world. The countries covered, albeit not equally well, include Arabia, China, Germany, France, Italy, Japan, Russia, Spain, West Africa, and Scandinavian and Latin American countries, as well as England and the U.S. The encyclopedia entries list authors from all over the world and include biographical and bibliographical information and plot summaries of selected novels. Although the **Guide to Crime Novels** lists among its faults several factual and bibliographical errors and reveals whodunit and how, it is especially worthy for its international coverage and the relative emphasis it places on writers and topics neglected in English-language secondary material. It definitely should be translated into English.

In 1971 there appeared two of the most important essay anthologies in the German language. **The Crime Novel (Der**

Kriminalroman), edited, in two volumes, by Jochen Vogt, contains forty essays, including those by Gerber and Alewyn, and several translations of English-language essays. In the same year, Yugoslavian critic Viktor Zmegac edited **The Good-Tempered Murder (Der wohltemperierte Mord)**, which contains twelve essays, including the other famous essay by Alewyn, one each by Bertolt Brecht, W.H. Auden, Edmund Wilson, and, interestingly enough, one each by Zmegac and one other Yugoslavian critic. These two anthologies were presumably planned independently of each other, for there are six essays which appear in both works.

Another boom year was 1973, in which several important books appeared, including the only German book-length study of the English spy novel, by Jens-Peter Becker (who, by the way, broke the criminous culture barrier by contributing to **Twentieth Century Crime and Mystery Writers**). The English Spy Novel (Der englische Spionageroman) traces the history of that genre and homes in on Buchan, Childers, Oppenheim, Compton Mackenzie, Ambler, Household, Michael Innes, le Carre, Deighton, Fleming, and William Haggard. Incidentally, this was the published version of Becker's dissertation. The same year Becker teamed up with his mentor, Professor Paul Buchloh, to write a series of connected essays on the detective novel. **The Detective Novel (Der Detektivroman)** contains chapters on systematic and historical topics such as rules of the game, spy novels, and the detective novel in Nazi Germany. It has since become the standard German introduction to the genre. In 1973 there also appeared a book on the uncanny in detective fiction and an encyclopedia-format book on popular culture with a long section on crime fiction.

Another standard treatment of the genre appeared in 1975: Ulrich Schulz-Buschhaus's **Forms and Ideologies of the Crime Novel (Formen und Ideologien des Kriminalromans)**. In this book Professor Schulz-Buschhaus applies the tools of literary and psychological criticism to authors Poe, Collins, Dickens, Hammett, and Chandler and to characters Arsene Lupin, Maigret, and the Fu Manchu-like Fantomas.

The 1970's also saw the publication of what might be considered a German version of Haycraft's **Art of the Mystery Story** in a return performance by the Buchloh/Becker team. Their **On the Trail of the Detective Story (Der Detektiverzaehlung auf der Spur,** 1977) is the first German anthology primarily of English-language essays on the subject. Many of the essays, including famous ones by Chesterton, Sayers, Ronald Knox, and others, were also in (and perhaps inspired by) Haycraft's anthology. Almost all of the English-language essays are well known, and only three essays out of the thirty chosen did not come from English.

In addition to these more general books, there appeared in the 1970's more specialized books. There were essay anthologies on Eric Ambler, Patricia Highsmith, Friedrich Durrenmatt, William Faulkner, and Simenon, studies on Christie, Simenon, Durrenmatt, Johannes Mario Simmel, and on fear in detective stories, and a small selection of books on the crime novel for use in schools as teachers' aids.

Since the seventies the most important work in German to appear is Peter Nusser's academic study, **The Crime Novel (Der Kriminalroman**, 1980). It is at once a systematic and historical introduction to the English-language genre, a survey of different subtopics, and an excellent review of German secondary literature. In fact, Nusser tips the balance and places too much emphasis on secondary literature and is at times arid and pretentious. Nevertheless, like **Reclam's Guide to Crime Novels**, Nusser's book is a wealth of information on the genre, albeit in a slim 186 pages.

CURIOSITIES

Among the many secondary works in German, a few stand out, not perhaps because they are important (though some are), but rather because they are odd, curious, or unique. As stated before, the general trend of German criticism is to evaluate the genre as a whole, but there are several excellent pieces on individual characters and authors. Professor Volker Neuhaus, of the University of Cologne, broke away from the academic pack by writing two essays on more compact subjects. His fine "Father Brown and Rabbi Small" (1975) and almost lyrical "Michael Innes: **From London Far**" (1977) are powerful, sophisticated literary studies on these topics. Hans Christoph Buch's "James Bond: Or, The Small Citizen with Weapons" ("James Bond, oder der Kleinbuerger in Waffen," 1961) is quite interesting, for without the help of the Bond film craze, which was a few years off, it anticipates the "popular culture" style of criticism which later became well known at the hands of George Grella and other English-language critics.

Then there are the **On** books. A Swiss paperback publisher, Diogenes, has a series of essay anthologies on authors, a number of whom are mystery writers. Of these, the best are **On Eric Ambler** (Ueber Eric Ambler, 1979), **On Simenon** (Ueber Simenon, 1978), and **On Patricia Highsmith** (Ueber Patricia Highsmith, 1980). The **On** books contain essays from French, Italian, German, and English sources, as well as little testimonial blurbs from world-famous personalities such as Alfred Hitchcock, Andre Gide, Henry Miller, and Federico Fellini. The essays are uniformly good, sometimes extremely good. The **On** books also feature a story or essay by the subject author, checklists of their work, radio and screen credits, and international bibliographies of secondary sources. In the case of **On Eric Ambler**, there is an autobiographical photo-sketch with commentary prepared by Ambler specifically for publisher Diogenes. The **On** books deserve translation into English, or perhaps a flattering sort of imitation by an enterprising English-language publisher.

An essay both unique and important is Willy Hass's "'Mysteries': From the Beginnings of the Crime Novel" ("'Mysteries'. Von den Anfaengen des Kriminalromans," 1958-1959). Haas's essay was probably the first in German to trace the history of English-language crime fiction from eighteenth-century Gothic mystery (in the strictest technical sense) fiction. He treats the work of Horace Walpole, M.G. ("Monk") Lewis, and Ann Radcliffe, as later German critics would also do. Another historical oddity is what is probably the second German monograph on the genre. Arthur Schimmelpfennig's sixteen-page **Contributions Toward the History of the Crime Novel** (1908), mentioned above, traces briefly the history of German, French, Italian, Russian, and English language crime fiction, provides notes on the crime novel in Portugal, Denmark, Norway, and Hungary, and sharply distinguishes among detective fiction, crime fiction, and cracksman stories. Quite perspicacious for such an early work.

Perhaps the most abstract, inaccessible piece ever written on the genre has been written in German. Siegfried Kracauer's work, **The Detective Novel: A Philosophical Treatise** (Der Detektiv-Roman. Ein Philosophischer Traktat, 1925), has deceptively simple chapter headings, such as "Hotel Lounge," "Detective," "Police," and "Criminals," but reader beware!! Kracauer uses Kantian and Hegelian concepts to argue that, in the novelistic world, Reason starts from a "negative ontology" signified by the lack of concrete Reality at the beginning of the story and gradually causes Reality to become fully determinate at the end. This presumably has to do with the sparseness of clues at the beginning and the fully explained solution at the end. The embodiment of Reason is, understandably enough, the detective. Professor Helmut Bonheim, chairman of the English Department at the University of Cologne, characterized Kracauer's book to me as a sort of monumental structure which everyone mentions and honors--and avoids. No one can read it, though it has only 125 pages. Professor Bonheim confessed that he had not got beyond page twenty-eight!

On the other hand, the Swiss critic Mary Hottinger is perhaps unique among German-language critics for taking an unabashedly fannish approach in her writing. In her three famous forewords to the even more famous trio of detective story anthologies--**Murder: Anglo Saxon Crime Stories (Mord. Angelsaechsische Kriminalgeschichten,** 1959), **More Murders (Mehr Morde,** 1961), and **Still More Murders (Noch mehr Morde,** 1963)--she takes her stance and her enthusiasm shows. She argues that murder is ever-growing in importance in the history of the crime novel, she likens the fall of the Great Detective to a "back to nature" movement, she staunchly defends the life and times of the detective story against curmudgeons and doomsayers, and she calls for a truce between rabid fans and those with snobbish tastes. Her writing is as knowledgeable as it is animated.

Last and perhaps least come the political/ideological critiques, those in which the crime novel is judged by standards quite foreign to its intent, and largely non-aesthetic. There are not many of these odd essays. In Nazi Germany, in 1940, Erich Thier argued in "On the Detective Novel" ("Ueber den Detektivroman") that the detective novel is a capitalistic phenomenon whose rationalism is harmful to belief in the **Fuhrer.** He further hinted that a truly German form would arise and revitalize the withering genre. In 1950 the socialist critic Harry Proll argued in "The Effective of Crime Novels" ("Die Wirkung der Kriminalromane") that the German popularity of crime fiction represents the needs of the masses to be liberated from capitalism. He then called for a socialist popular literature that would be as fun to read as capitalist crime fiction. Oddly enough, Proll is one of the most well-read critics when it comes to English-language crime fiction; he is also the only German critic I know to mention Fu Manchu. Oddly again, his article was first published in the **Magazine for Political Psychology and Sexual Economy.**

Feminist Erika Dingeldey takes E.S. Gardner, Chandler, and Spillane to task in "Who Is the Guilty One? Aspects of the Woman in the American Crime Novel" ("Wer ist der Schuldige? Aspekte der Frau im amerikanischen Kriminalroman," 1969). She charges these writers with portraying women as unrealistic, nymphomaniacal, and dependent upon the male. She spares Hammett, however, because of his positive Nora Charles character. If Dingeldey finds these writers the most chauvinistic and sexually offensive, it's quite probable she never read any of the Ted Mark books.

Finally, the Russian critic I.I. Revzin gives a technical semiotic critique of Agatha Christie's novels in "Towards a Semiotic Analysis of the Detective Novel: Example--The Novels of Agatha Christie" ("Zur semiotischen Analyse des Detektivromans am Beispiel der Romane Agatha Christies," 1964). Although semiotics is not a non-aesthetic critical approach as are the Nazi, socialist, and feminist approaches, it can be considered an aesthetic **ideology.** Revzin discusses the character types frequently found in Christie's novels and then gives some competition to the unreadable Kracauer monument as he cryptically sums up the detective novel: "On the level of the aesthetic symbol-system of detective fiction ... a construction is presented in which no sort of reality lies behind the symbols." I suppose he's saying the detective novel is unrealistic.

The German contribution to the secondary literature on crime fiction has been dominated by an intellectual, analytic, and to a lesser extent, historical approach. Partly because of their distance from the hubs of criminous literary activity they choose to write about, German critics have given some extremely intriguing and extremely abstract insights into the English-language genre, seeing into areas our critics might be too close to see. Where our critics write about the trees, German critics write about the forest. On the other hand, one would like to see, if at all possible, more work on German crime fiction, more bibliographical activity, perhaps some specialized periodicals, more studies of writers, characters, and subgenres, and more fannish, non-academic, non-professional writinig (these three not being necessarily co-extensive). Perhaps these "on the other hand" comments are due to my being influenced by the Anglo-American approach, but it is interesting to note that all of these neglected byways are flourishing in German sf/fantasy and comic-book criticism.

[1] Note on the Alewyn-Gerber controversy. The following gives the bibliographical information on the articles involved in the controversy, in partial chronological order (the last three appearances were in 1971):

Alwyn, Richard. "The Mystery of the Detective Novel" ("Das Raetsel des Detektivromans"). In A. Frise, ed., **Definitionen** (Frankfurt: Klostermann, 1963), pp. 117-136.
Gerber, Richard. "Criminal Fiction and the Crime Novel" ("Verbrechensdichtung und Kriminalroman"). **Neue Deutsche Hefte** 111:3:101-117, 1966.
Alewyn, Richard. "Anatomy of the Detective Novel" ("Anatomie des Detektivromans"). **Die Zeit** 47 and 48, November 22 and 29, 1968, Literature Section, pp. 10f.
Gerber, Richard. Revised version of "Criminal Fiction and the Crime Novel" in Jochen Vogt, ed., **Der Kriminalroman**, vol. 2 (Munich: Fink, 1971), pp. 404-420.
Alewyn, Richard. Revised version of "The Mystery of the Detective Novel," re-titled as "The Beginnings of the Detective Novel" ("Die Anfaenge des Detektivromans"). In Zmegac, Viktor, ed., **The Good-Tempered Murder (Der Wohltemperierte Mord)**, Frankfurt: Athenaeum Verlag, 1971, pp. 185-202.
_____. Expanded version of "Anatomy of the Detective Novel" in Vogt, **Der Kriminalroman**, volume 2, pp. 372-404.

The Crime Story in Sweden

K. Arne Blom

Interest in detective and crime fiction in Sweden goes back to the nineteenth century. Many of the best English, American, and French writers were translated during the last quarter of the century, often soon after publication in their own countries. Some of the worst were also translated. Stories by Poe, Wilkie Collins, Gaboriau, Conan Doyle, and others appeared in Sweden, together with tales about Nick Carter, who in these years was not as violent as he is today.

Even in the early part of the nineteenth century there was a strong Swedish interest in real-life crime and in tales of horror. The memoirs of Vidocq, the chief of the Sureté, were translated into Swedish a year after their publication in France, and the work of the German writer of Gothic horror stories E.T A. Hoffman was also much read and enjoyed. The writer who in many respects must be regarded as the father of Swedish detective fiction was much influenced by Hoffmann. This was Carl Jonas Love Almqvist (1793-1866). In 1851 Almqvist came under suspicion of having committed murder by poison. He left Sweden before he could be charged and settled in the United States. In 1865 he returned to Europe but, not daring to return to Sweden, he ended his life in Germany. His **Drottningens juvelsmycke (The Queen's Diamond Ornament)**, published in 1834, might be called a crime novel or a political thriller. But the work that truly establishes Almqvist as the father of Swedish detective fiction is a short story written in 1838 entitled "Skallnora kvarn" ("The Mill of Skallnora"). This is a strange mixture of Gothic, romantic story, and suspense thriller. It is not likely that Almqvist knew of Poe's work, and his main influence was Hoffmann. The story is about a poisoning, and the action is fast and violent. There is a whodunit element in "Skallnora kvarn", but more strongly present is the feeling of psychology entering the crime story.

"Skallnora kvarn" was a good short story. The first crime novel of quality is **Doktor Glas (Doctor Glass)** [1905]. Its author, Hjalmar Soderberg (1869-1941) was a "straight" novelist, rather than a crime writer. In Sweden, as elsewhere, there is a difference between "real novelists" and "crime novelists," a ridiculous distinction because the difference is really between good and bad writers. **Doktor Glas**, however, cannot be characterized as anything else but a splendid psychological crime novel, revealing the inner factors that might force a human being to commit murder. This fine-tuned book about melancholy, loneliness, and dreams is a brilliant piece of prose, still living thanks to Soderberg's graceful style and his skill in rendering a tender fin-de-siecle melancholy.

A number of other books appeared near the beginning of the

twentieth century which are now of purely historical interest. The basic reason for the failure of these books was that the writers were trying to copy foreign books, renaming the characters and calling them Swedes. A distinctively Swedish literary tradition was missing. Nevertheless, the year 1893 is of some historical interest. In that year Prins Pierre published his **Stockholm-detektiven (The Stockholm Detective)**. Behind this royal pen-name was to be found Fredrik Lindholm. The book is almost unreadable today, but still it was the first full-length Swedish crime novel, and it introduced the first detective in Swedish crime fiction. His name was Fridolf Hammar. At this period the Danes and Norwegians who wanted to read detective fiction were more happily situated. In Norway Stein Riverton wrote a great many crime stories, and the books were read and loved outside his own country. Much better as a writer was Palle Rosenkrantz, whose work is still highly enjoyable. A short story by him, "A Sensible Course of Action," is included in Hugh Greene's **More Rivals of Sherlock Holmes**.

Perhaps it was inevitable that it should be Sherlock Holmes who liberated the Swedish crime writers. What may be called one of the first victims of the Holmes syndrome was a clergyman, Frans Oscar Wagman (1849-1913). Under his own name he wrote some ambitious historical novels which are now unreadable. Using the pen-name Sture Stig, he wrote some amusing pastiches about a Holmes who is hopelessly inefficient and solves his cases only by luck. These were first published in a Swedish newspaper, and then in 1908 the first collection appeared, **Sherlock Holmes i ny belysning (New Light on Sherlock Holmes)**. Stig, during a visit to England, meets Dr. Watson while visiting a manor house and persuades Watson to tell him the true facts about life in Baker Street. It was, Watson says, unbearable. The rooms were dirty and were often visited by the most disgusting characters. Holmes's eternal creaking on the violin was appalling. "Had I not taken chloral I would most certainly have been driven mad." Watson says also that during Holmes's experiments with different poisons the doctor was in constant fear of his life. The detective is too simple-minded to understand his own stupidity, and his cases are mostly solved by accident. After leaving England Stig stays in touch with Watson, and in correspondence the good doctor tells him enough for a second volume of stories. **Nya Sherlock Holmes-historier (New Sherlock Holmes Stories)**, which appeared in 1910, is not as good as the first volume, but the stories as a whole will stand comparison with any among the hundreds of pastiches that gently mock the Holmes canon.

In 1913 Samuel August Duse (1873-1933) made his debut. He was to become the first writer of real skill and importance who produced nothing but crime stories. His books were tremendously popular, and he was called "Sweden's own Conan Doyle." The Swedish writer Ivar Lo-Johansson in one of his autobiographical novels mentions the novels of Duse in a manner that makes one believe that these detective stories were found in as many Swedish homes of the times as the Bible, the Book of Hymns, and the Catechisms. Many papers published short stories by Duse, and his books were constantly reprinted. In his time, Duse dominated the crime fiction scene.

He wrote in all more than a dozen novels, starting with **Stilettkappen (The Stiletto Cane)**. His private detective is named Leo Carring, who in this first book's first chapter explains why Holmes was such a humbug.

It is impossible not to get the impression that his

activity as a consulting detective is to him a sort of hazardous game, in which he is constantly lucky. He is always guessing right, although he might just as well be completely wrong. Too often it is pure chance that gives him the leads and indications he needs. One single false guess concerning one tiny detail, one single mistaken deduction, would have sent him off on the wrong track.

No doubt it was natural for Duse to invent a fantasy Holmes who was an impossible **ubermensch** to praise by contrast to his own master detective, but before long Duse falls into the trap of letting Carring think and act as a Swedish copy of Holmes. These were long books, but they were well-written and the problems in them were cleverly presented and solved. The books also contain a lot of contemporary documentation, so that they do give an idea of the way people behaved, thought, and dressed in the period. Among Duse's best books are **Doktor Smirnos dagbok (The Diary of Doctor Smirnov)** of 1918 and **Fallet Dagmar (The Dagmar Case)** of 1925, the latter of which is based on an actual crime.

The spirit of Holmes is present when one is reading Duse. When reading Gunnar Serner (1886-1947), one feels a more French influence. Serner was from Lund, but had to leave his studies at the university because of financial problems. He abandoned Sweden. settling first in Monte Carlo and then later on the island of Bornholm, which is part of Denmark. While in Monte Carlo, trying to make a living by playing the tables, he began to write, and in 1914 his first two books appeared. I **hasardens huvudstad (In the Capital of Gambling)** and **Herr Collins affarer i London** (translated into English in 1924 as **The London Adventures of Mr. Collins**) are very charming works. The book about Mr. Collins was the first in a series inspired by the Arsene Lupin stories.

Gunnar Serner wrote as Frank Heller. He was a brilliant stylist and had a talent for telling entertaining stories. He was to become one of the most loved and read writers in Sweden, and he produced more than fifty books, novels, short stories, travel books, and a delightful autobiography. As far as I know, he was the first Swedish crime writer to be translated into English, appearing both in Britain and the United States. Approximately half of his books were crime stories, and according to his autobiography he regarded them as "travesties or pastiches on the popular crime-genre." Maurice Leblanc, who was also popular in Sweden, meant a great deal to Heller, but he is by no means a mere imitator. His best books are **Storhertigens finanser** (1915), translated in 1924 as **The Grand Duke's Finances**, and the two sequels to it, and **Kejsarens gamla klader** (1918), which was translated in 1923 as **The Emperor's Old Clothes** in the U.S. and **The Chinese Coats** in Britain. Heller also wrote books about a Jewish psychoanalyst, Joseph Zimmertur from Amsterdam, which are more like whodunits. He remains highly readable and very entertaining. Most Swedish crime writers of the period were pedestrian, but Heller was a virtuoso, a crane among sparrows.

Julius Regis was less talented than Serner/Heller, but he became equally popular. His real name was Julius Petersson (1889-1925), and he earned his living as a proof-reader on a daily paper. He was influenced by the Nick Carter tales and other fast-moving suspense stories. His hero, the "problem hunter" Wallion, also makes some clever deductions. His books might be called an unlikely synthesis of elements in Nick Carter and in Sherlock Holmes.

The hero's full name is Maurice Wallion, crime reporter at the biggest daily in Stockholm, who became world-famous when he worked for a French paper and there not only wrote about crime and criminals but captured them as well. Wallion is an idealized Regis, and the stories, which are full of fantastic exaggerations, present a curious blend of thriller and whodunit. Wallion is at home not only in Stockholm and Paris, but all over Latin America as well. Most of the criminals he fights are international crooks, and of course he always defeats them. **Det bla sparet (The Blue Track)**, Regis's first book, was published in 1916, and like some of the others is readable today, although the modern reader is likely to find some of the effects comic. In all, Regis wrote fifteen books, two of which were translated into English: **Kopparhuset** (1918, as **The Copper House** (1923), and **Nr 13 Toroni** (1919), as **No. 13 Toroni** (1923). Unhappily, these are not among his best books.

Duse wrote about a Stockholm that felt and smelt rather like the London of Holmes, even if one has to admit that much of contemporary Stockholm was present. Heller set most of his books in international surroundings, and so did Regis. But where were the Genuine Swedish crime writers, those writing about typical Swedes and their way of life? Well, with one exception they are difficult to discover. The exception is Fanny Alving (1874-1955). Her single crime novel was **Josefssons pa Drottninggatan (The Josefssons at Queen's Street)**, published in 1918. It is an entertaining and even lovable book, and in it appears the first Swedish woman detective, Jullan Eriksson.

Few other writers in this period call for detailed discussion. One popular writer was August Jansson, who was hardly able to write readable Swedish and totally incapable of giving a spark of life to his characters, who sound like bureaucratic formulas when they talk. In the thirties, however, three newspapermen and one woman brought a promise of something new to the Swedish crime story. They all wrote well, and their books were something more than echoes of foreign crime stories.

Sture Appelberg (1885-?) in 1931 wrote **Obligationsmysteriet (The Mystery of the Bonds)**, which begins well but offers an unsatisfactory ending. His best book is **De doda skeppens vik (Bay of the Dead Ships)** of 1933, which offers an unsatisfactory ending. His best book is **De doda skeppens vik (Bay of the Dead Ships)** of 1933, which offers three dimensional characters and believable scenes, so that we really care what happens in the story. The most talented of the three men was Yngve Hedvall. He wrote only two crime novels, but they give him a place on the Swedish Parnassus. **Tragedin i Villa Siola (The Tragedy in Villa Siola)** of 1934 is a clever and well constructed variant of **The Murder of Roger Ackroyd**. It remains one of the best dozen crime stories written in Sweden. His other book, **Khedives gava (The Riddle of the Khedive)** is also very good, and the sad thing about Hedvall is that he wrote no more crime stories.

Torsten Sandberg (1900-1947) wrote four books, all still very much worth reading. His characters are really Swedes, his settings are strongly national, and the Swedish disposition and temper are very much present in such good novels as **De sju Natternas mysterium (The Mystery of the Seven Nights)** of 1933 and **Tragedin i dimman (A Tragedy in the Fog)** which appeared a year later.

And so to the woman. Kjerstin Goransson-Ljungman (1901-1971) published her first book in 1939, **27 sekundmeter sno (Storm and Snow)**. It is and will remain a pearl among Swedish crime novels. Ten people are isolated in a small cottage in the Swedish Alps during a snow storm. One is murdered, and from there the story goes on in a way that makes the reading of it a true pleasure. ... och bjuder jag tackelset falla (**May the Veil Fall**) of 1940 was not as good as the first book, but it was still good enough to make it clear that Goransson-Ljungman was the first queen of Swedish crime fiction. These four writers also showed that Swedish detective fiction was ready to leave the cradle. It should be emphasized again that until World War II Swedish crime stories, with these few exceptions, were very inferior articles, traditional whodunits, poorly written and obviously derivative from the best foreign masters. Apart from **Doktor Glas**, there was not a single psychological crime story, there were no hardboiled mysteries in the American vein, and of course there were no police procedurals. And it is perhaps a criticism of the audience that Goransson-Ljungman had little success with her books. She continued to write, and to write well, but she never reached the large audience that her qualities deserved.

With the forties all this changed. The period began a Golden Age for the crime story in Sweden, an age that lasted for some twenty years. The foreground figures were Stieg Trenter and Vic Suneson. I have been told that Stieg Trenter (1914-1967) was the model for the Swedish newspaper correspondent in Evelyn Waugh's **Scoop**. He was the only Swedish journalist in Abyssinia at the time the Italians marched in, and he knew Waugh. But at that time Trenter was not Trenter.

His name was Stig Johansson. He was a young man who wanted to become a journalist, but at the daily where he worked, **Stockholms-Tidningen**, there were already three reporters named Johansson. The newest and youngest was ordered to change his name. He had just read **Trent's Last Case**, and Trent had a certain ring to it. The authorities, however, insisted that it should be Trenter. His first name is due to a printing mistake by which Stig became Stieg. As Stieg Trenter he had become a star reporter and written plays for the radio before his first book, **Ingen kan hejda doden (Nobody Can Stop Death)**, was published in 1943, in collaboration with a friend who withdrew from the project. The work showed a promise fulfilled by two books in the following year.

Som man ropar (Cry for It) is a thriller, a well-written and well-balanced spy story with a wonderful twist at the end. Sweden has produced few spy stories, and Trenter's is one of the best. It is also a good book about Sweden during World War II, a book which says a lot about moods and fears in a neutral country.

The other book that year was **Farlig fafanga (Dangerous Vanity)**, in which Trenter's main character appears for the first time. His name is Harry Friberg, and by profession he is a photographer. He is tall, friendly and pleasant, and a bit naive. Trenter was skilled enough to create a figure who seems to be a detective genius but is actually a quite ordinary man who finds himself involved in murder cases. In the following year Trenter introduced another character--policeman Vesper Johnson, CID superintendent. He appears first in **I tag rod (Red Today)**. He is small, eccentric, sharp-witted, and loves food. So does Friberg. They compliment each other admirably.

For nearly two decades Stieg Trenter dominated Swedish detective fiction, so much so that his name was almost synonymous with it. He was a brilliant writer, and it was very much thanks to him that the genre got a life-giving injection. Trenter was a clever constructor of plots and intrigues and an excellent prose writer, so his goods do not date. He was also a good--almost lyrical--describer of Stockholm, on of the three or four best among all Swedish authors in writing about the capital. And last, but not least, Trenter was a fine psychologist who created very plausible characters. His criminals are not committing crimes **pour l'art**, and the explanations of their motives are so skilled that they become touchingly human. **Traff i helfigur** (**The Good Marksman**) of 1948 is a good example of this. His greatest weakness is his female characters. Most of them are cliches, adventurous and eager blondes. But still, until 1960, a bad book by Trenter was an exception. After that his work declined, although he was still much read. His wife, Ulla Trenter (1936-), wrote most of his last book in the year he died. Since then she has continued to write about Harry Friberg. One wishes she would not.

The second giant of the period made his debut in 1948, although he was a giant with obvious limitations. His name was Sune Lundquist (1918-1975), but he used the name Vic Suneson. He considered using the name Victoria, since he had been told that books by female crime writers sold more copies, but he fortunately kept his sex. Suneson was not a great stylist, nor did he create many interesting characters, but he had high narrative skill. The most important thing about him was that he was a bold and interesting experimenter, always trying to do something new. When he succeeded, the result was splendid. One of his most interesting experiments is **Ar jag mordaren?** (**Did I Kill?**) of 1953.

It is sometimes claimed also that Suneson was the first Swede to write police procedural stories, but this is only half-true. He wrote about good, honest policemen who were capable of doing their jobs and did not have to consult private or amateur detectives. He also described police routine work in an authentic way, and he knew about technical details. But in the end his books are always traditional puzzles. The last chapter always gathers together the suspects, reveals what really happened, exposes the murderer. This is not realism, and in Suneson's hands it is sometimes pure melodrama. But such excellent books as **Fredagen den 14:e** (**Friday the 14th**) of 1960 and **Skarvor betyder lycka** (**Broken Glass Is Happiness**) of the following year are proofs that he could have written realistic police procedural mysteries. His policemen--first Inspector Kjell Myhrman, later Inspector O.P. Nilsson when Myhrman is transferred--are rather gray and blurred in their outlines, but this helps to make them more believable police figures. Syneson also described milieus well, and his descriptions of Stockholm have a documentary flavor. His last books were painfully weak, but his best work will always be regarded with respect.

One cannot say the same of Maria Lang (1914-), a pseudonym of Dagmar Lange. She is sometimes mentioned as the queen of Swedish crime novelists, and three of her books have been published in English translations. Her first story appeared in 1949 and became an immediate success with readers, perhaps because of the piquant lesbian motive. In general, however, she must be called an uninteresting hybrid of Agatha Christie and Mary Roberts Rinehart.

Much more original are three books by Peter Gunby and Staffan Tjerneld (1901-). Gunby, a pen-name for Thore Ericson, wrote only one book, and Tjerneld only two. Tjerneld's first was **Brott i sol** (**Crime in the Sun**), published in 1947, and the second was **Rod amaryllis** (**Red Amaryllis**), of 1951. They are especially interesting for the development they show in the psychological crime story.

In 1954 Hans Krister Ronblom (1901-1965) published his first book, **Dod bland de doda** (**Dead Among the Dead**). Ronblom was a political journalist, and his ten novels give a very believable picture of life in the Swedish country areas.

If Trenter's books were proof that the crime story is a useful tool if one wants to document the life of the city, the books of H.K., as he was called, are as much a proof that the crime story can be used to describe the changing world and people of his time. H.K. told about the transformation of Sweden, of an agricultural society changed to an industrial one. These are sociological accounts of Sweden, and also excellent crime novels. They give life to the fifties, so that the reader can really smell the decade and believe in it.

His sleuth, the teacher Paul Kennet, a pipe smoker with a personal relationship to his pipes, is a calm man who uses his intellect and does not walk around hitting people. This sympathetic figure might be called a combination of Rip Kirby and Maigret. Kennet smells and feels the atmosphere, and when he is analyzing the reciprocal action of humans this enables him to understand what happens, and why. He wrote about boarding houses in the country, temperance lodges, small factories, small towns, ordinary people. His best books are **Hostvind och djupa vatten (Wind in Autumn and Water Deep)** of 1955, **Tala om rep (Speak about Ropes)** of 1958, and **Krans at den skona (A Garland for the Beauty)**, which appeared in 1960. They may seem moody, but they give a true picture of the Swedish temper. Since H.K. wrote with high ambition, these are very good novels as well as crime stories. They are well plotted, and the psychological portraits of the characters are convincing.

During the forties the American hard-boiled school found its way to Sweden. Hammett had been translated a little earlier, and Chandler followed him. Soon came Mickey Spillane, Bart Spicer, Thomas B. Dewey, Thomas Walsh. Naturally, some Swedish writers tried to create a national hard-boiled crime story. Only one succeeded, mainly because the hard-boiled school is inseparably connected to American society. Anders Jonason (1925-), however, did write successful books in this vein, so that the readers experienced violence without feeling that people were beaten to death every second hour in the back streets of Stockholm. In **Mord med mera (Murder and Much More)**, of 1953, and **Mordaren kommer strax (The Murderer Will Soon Be Here)** of 1956 he wrote successfully about tough characters in Stockholm and the way they lived.

Jonason wrote only four books, and Arne Stigson, a pen-name for Arne Malmberg (1918-) wrote no more than three. The second of these, **Den resandes ensak (The Voyager's Own Business)** of 1957 is an almost perfect psychological crime story, as good as any of its British or American equivalents. So are the best books of Kerstin Ekman (1933-), who began by experimenting with the crime story, but then turned to straight novels. She is now a member of the Swedish Academy. **Dodsklockan (Bell of Death)**, 1963, about an accident during an elk hunt, is one of the best Swedish crime stories.

Among what might be called Swedish homespun are the books by Helena Poloni, the pen-name of Ingegerd Stadener (1903-1968). She wrote conventional whodunits, but her characters are real people. She wrote very lyrically about small-town life, and one feels how much she must have loved this world which she describes with nostalgic affection. Jan Ekstrom (1923-) wrote his first book, **Doden fyller ar (Death's Birthday)** in 1961. He is Sweden's best creator of locked-room puzzles. If they could have read Swedish, John Dickson Carr and Clayton Rawson might have been slightly jealous of Ekstrom's puzzles and locked-room constructions in **Alkistan (The Eel's Coffin)** of 1967, and in **Dodsdansen (Dance of Death)**, published in the same year. As pure puzzles, Ekstrom's books are successful, but anybody who feels that crime stories should also be novels will be disappointed by them. His characters are paper thin, and as a stylist he is as stimulating as S.S. Van Dine.

During this Golden Age of Swedish crime fiction the puzzle story was the most popular kind of book. There were some good psychological crime novels, and a few well-balanced syntheses of whodunits and psychological stories. It was the police procedural, however, that gave life to another Golden Age.

This began in 1965 when Maj Sjowall (1935-) and Per Wahloo (1926-1975) published their first book in the series, "The Story of a Crime," which was to consist of ten titles. From the beginning they made it clear that they would use the police procedural story as a tool for analyzing the Swedish welfare state. They did this on a Marxist basis. The ten books about Martin Beck and his colleagues can be divided into three categories.

In the first three (the first was **Roseanna**, translated under the same title in 1967), Beck is rather like a Maigret-type of policeman. He reflects upon criminals and tries to understand their actions in relation to their society. In the four following books the police team operates in the 87th Precinct manner. The criminals are seen through the eyes of several different policemen. In the last three books Sjowall and Wahloo became truly independent of other police procedural writers. They found their own style. The books became longer, more densely plotted, and blacker in their analyses of society. The books are believable, and nobody in them becomes a criminal just for the sake of the plot, but it must be said that the picture of Swedish society is often exaggerated. These ten books by Sjowall and Wahloo are political fingers with nails made of humanity, although the nails are missing in the last three books, which have become too doctrinal.

It is strange that so few other Swedish writers tried to write like Sjowall and Wahloo after they achieved international fame. However, they certainly stimulated other writers with the result that the Swedish crime story is flourishing. In Denmark there are two crime writers of the highest competence--Anders Bodelsen and Paul Orum. Norway is less happily placed, but the situation seems hopeful. In Sweden twenty to thirty native crime novels are published yearly, and certainly four or five of them are as good as many books published in the U.K. and the U.S.

Jean Bolinder (1935-) is one of the most interesting among the recent writers. He published his first book in 1967, **Skulle jag sorja da (If I Should Mourn)**, and it became an immediate critical success. His early works were in the traditional puzzle style, but he has always been interested in experimenting. He began with a couple, husband and wife, as his central characters, and then abandoned them for a taxi-driver. Gradually Bolinder's books have become less whodunits and more accounts of lost souls. A fine example of what he can do at his best is **Livet ar Langt (Life Is Long)**, of 11973, a book which echoes the theme of a play by August Strindberg.

Jan Olof Ekholm (1931-) also uses an anti-hero, a journalist named Goran Sandhal, who has a wonderful talent for tripping over the truth and not recognizing it until it is too late. Ekholm's book often scourge, in a very funny way, the life of small towns. His **Pang, du ar do (Bang, You're Dead)**, of 1969, is a delightful combination of crime novel, military farce, and tragi-comic novel. **Dod i skonhet (She Died a Beauty)** of 1970 reveals many painful truths about being a foreigner in Sweden.

Olov Svedelid (1932-) was one of the first writers to produce successful police procedurals which did not copy Sjowall and Wahloo. His first books were thrillers with a newspaperman as the hero. **Samtal fran en dod (Call from the Dead)** of 1970 is very good, but there is a breakthrough in his work with the stories about the policeman Roland Hassel and his colleagues. **Anmald forsvunnen (Reported Missing)** of 1972, in particular, shows Stockholm as a frighteningly inhuman city. With fine journalistic sharpness and much skill Svedelid shows crime on different levels in Swedish society.

Anders Hellen (1909-) is the pen-name of the former clergyman Carl Greek, who wrote his whodunits in the fifties. They are still very readable, but his best book was published in 1973, **En ljugande malm (For Whom the Bells Are Lying)**. This tory about a crime committed in a medieval monastery combines religious and juridical morals. It is the work of a virtuoso, and as historical crime story it is a masterpiece.

Sven Sormark (1923-) wrote his first psychological crime novel in 1968, **Vack inte Marie (Don't Wake Marie)**, a brilliant study of a criminal's mind, and has continued to write very interesting books. He might sometimes remind the reader of both Georges Simenon and Friedrich Durrenmatt. Tord Hubert (1933-) started by combining the hard-boiled and the humorous crime story. His second book, **Mord och och morske man (The Brave and the Dead)**, of 1967, is one of the best comic crime stories produced in Sweden. His later books are political thrillers, and **Den andres dod (Another's Death)**, of 1976, is of the highest international competence, and probably the best thriller written in Sweden.

Olle Hogstrang (1934-) writes political thrillers and police procedurals. The thrillers are preferable, and the first one, **Maskerat brott** (translated as **On the Prime Minister's Account** in 1973), combines his two interests. **Skulden** (1973), translated in 1975 as **The Debt**, is a spy novel, a melancholy and beautiful book about houman weaknesses, dreams, and hard realities.

K. Arne Blom's (1946-) first three police procedurals are set in Lund, a Swedish university town of moderate size. They deal with problems facing the students at a modern university. **Sanningens ogonblick** of 1974, translated as **The Moment of Truth** in 1977, shows, as does **Valdets triumf (The Triumph of Violence** of 1975, how violence creates further violence. His books deal with the expectations and fears of modern people in a troubled society. He has also written a trilogy of psychological crime stories and a series of police procedurals set in the future.

Ulf Durling (1940-) had his first book published in 1971. It mocked the whole genre and was considered very amusing by many people. Perhaps he is best, however, when writing psychological stories, and a good example of his skill is **Annars dor man (If Nort—You Die)** of 1977.

K.G. Mathiason, a pen-name for Bennie Liljenfors (1939-) is another talented writer of psychological crime novels. His three books--**Alskaren (The Lover), Mordaren (The Murderer)**, and **Ranaren (The Robber)**, published yearly from 1976--are all very good.

Ladies last--and at the moment it must be said that there are few good women crime writers in Sweden. Jenny Berthelius (1923-) is undoubtedly the best. She has been writing since 1968, and **Den heta sommaren (The Hot Summer)** of 1969, and **Mannen med lien (The Man with the Scythe)** of 1970 are cleverly plotted crime novels about the fears and struggles of ordinary people. If Sjowall and Wahloo had little direct influence, they inspired other Swedes to develop and experiment with the crime story. There is good ground for such efforts in Sweden, because the reading audience is large. Each year some two hundred crime stories are published, of course most of them being translations from the U.K. and the U.S.

The problem for Swedish crime writers is that comparatively few people can read the language in which they weite. When one compares much of what appears in other countries with Swedish books, it is plain that at least a handful of the country's crime writers deserve a fate more kind than that of reaching an audience only of their own countrymen.

To sum up, the international situation is well reflected in Sweden. There are now few good writers of traditional whodunits, many excellent psychological novelists, and some good writers of police procedural stories. The traditional limitations of detective fiction are slowly being eroded in Sweden. The lover of the pure whodunit may not like it, but this is what is happening. One should not exaggerate and claim that Swedish crime fiction is today the best in the world, but much of it is as good as that written elsewhere and deserves an international audience.

IT'S ABOUT CRIME by Marvin Lachman

NOTES ON RECENT READING

Dodd, Mead has been responsible for most of the recent excitement in mystery publishing. They do the Dan Mallett mysteries of Frank Parrish, and these are about as good as anything being published these days. When non-mystery reading friends or relatives ask me to recommend an author, I usually suggest Dick Francis. Now, many of them have gone through his works, so I think I'll recommend Parrish to them.

His series character is a poacher in the English countryside, and his unusual occupation and odd mixture of morality and immorality make him especially interesting. He is a dropout from a banking career who has chosen to live close to nature and usually outside the law. Still, he needs money for his mother, who should have a hip transplant because of severe arthritis but won't agree to being hospitalized under the British National Health system. After four books, this motivation (and Mrs. Mallett's impairment) is becoming a bit tiresome. Otherwise, these books are awfully good. Parrish is an excellent storyteller who builds up suspense deftly. He involves Mallett in murders in plausible ways, forcing him to solve them because he is suspected, albeit not guilty. His nature descriptions place you at the scene. You feel the chill morning air and hear the insects buzzing in your ears.

There have been four Mallett books, all published in hardcover by Dodd, Mead. The first three have just been reprinted in paper by Perennial Library. Here is the list for you completists: **Fire in the Barley** (1977); **Sting of the Honeybee** (1978); **Snare in the Dark** (1981); and **Bait on the Hook** (1983). You won't be sorry you sought out Frank Parrish, whether in hardcover or paperback.

Also from Dodd, Mead, perhaps to coincide with the series on public television, is a reprinting of **The Father Brown Omnibus**. This generous volume of 993 pages has 51 stories, including "The Vampire of the Village," the story that does not appear in any of the individual Chesterton books. It also includes a fine introduction by Auberon Waugh. I found the TV series a bit disappointing, and if you did also, try the original. They're much better; Father Brown works better in the mind rather than in full view on screen.

Dodd, Mead has now launched a paperback series with reprints by some of their most popular hardcover authors: Ursula Curtiss, Evelyn Berckman, Rae Foley, and Velda Johnston. Due in the future are McGivern, Pentecost, and others. Especially interesting in the first batch is Berckman's **Do You Know This Voice?** (1960). This is a very suspenseful kidnapping story and well worth reading. I hope Dodd, Mead will do that author's much better first novel, **The Evil of Time.** Equally readable is the Johnston entry, **The House Above Hollywood** (1968), with its likable narrator and well-depicted Southern California scene. Johnston is still writing, making her one of the longest-lasting authors around. I found a story by Velda Johnston in the April 1938 issue of **Breezy Stories!**

Meanwhile, Dodd, Mead continues to publish its standbys, like Michael Innes, but they are also publishing some new authors, two of whom are members of what I like to think of as the "doomsday" school of suspense writing. **Blue Flame,** by Joseph Gilmore, tells of the efforts of a British agent to prevent Libyan terrorists from blowing up an LNG (Liquified Natural Gas) supertanker in Boston harbor. The impact would be equal to 100 Hiroshima blasts. I'd have enjoyed this a bit more if the MI5 agent, Baldwin, wasn't such a bumbler. Also, in a book that is not satire I was jarred by lines like "Baldwin cried as he grabbed the dispatch in one aching hand and a soggy egg roll in the other." This is just one example of the appetite of probably the first spy in fiction who has a love affair with cold moo goo gai pan.

Better written and more off the beaten track is Carl A. Posey's **Kiev Footprint,** in which a science reporter investigates an international plot involving a satellite and cosmonaut stranded in space. There is the possibility that the satellite's re-entry will be used as a dangerous ploy to heat up the Cold War. The enormity of the situation is never entirely made believable, but this is still an exciting first novel.

Avon has reprinted a delightful old book, Christopher Morley's **Haunted Bookshop** (1919), adding illustrations by Douglas Gorsline. Set just after World War I, it's mystery elements are relatively minor, but decidedly present. What makes **The Haunted Bookshop** memorable is its love of books as conveyed by the Brooklyn bookstore owner and raconteur, Roger Mifflin. A self-styled "practitioner in bibliotherapy," he analogizes book sellers to doctors, saying the former prescribe books to heal minds. Mifflin even tells us what a "librocubicularist" is. It's a person fond of reading in bed. I suspect that most readers of this publication love books as much as I do. If so, they will probably find this book irresistible. They will also enjoy its depiction of a long-gone, simpler era and its early satire of the advertising industry.

Though all his mystery writing and editing was ghosted, Alfred Hitchcock belongs in our genre because for fifty years he directed mystery films. That is an understatement, because no one came even close to "Hitch" in directorial excellence in the suspense field. **The Lodger, The Lady Vanishes, The 39 Steps, Shadow of a Doubt, Spellbound, Strangers on a Train, Vertigo, North by Northwest, Psycho, Frenzy** .... The number seems endless.

Little, Brown & Co. has recently published Donald Spoto's unauthorized, albeit very exhaustive, biography, **The Dark Side of Genius: The Life of Alfred Hitchcock.** It is $20, but it's worth it, containing 555 pages, many photographs, and a great deal of information. As the subtitle implies, Spoto has written a psycho-biography designed to show that Hitchcock had many mental quirks which prevented him from having meaningful relationships with most people. He also emphasizes that Hitchcock had many unsatisfied sexual longings which led to his practical jokes and abuse of some of his beautiful blonde stars, such as Madeline Carrol, Joan Fontaine, and, especially, Tippi Hedren, who came from (and went back into) obscurity to star in **The Birds** and **Marnie.**

The precise documentation of these charges and of the one that near the end of his career Hitchcock made an improper proposal to a studio typist is minimal. Still, the weight of evidence implies that the allegations are true. It does seem that Spoto dwells upon this at too great length. Similarly, he seems overly anxious to prove that Hitchcock was a liar at times. Spoto is probably at his worst, among his moments of supposition, when he claims (without evidence) that the director was repelled at the pregnancy of his wife. He ascribes the following **thoughts** to him regarding her appearance: "... distended, bloated—beginning, perhaps he thought, to resemble himself." I prefer what Hitchcock actually did say regarding the birth of daughter Patricia. "I nearly died of the suspense."

Spoto knows films and does a masterful job of interweaving the circumstances under which each film was made with Hitchcock's life at the time. Thus we get a rare picture of the English film industry in its early days. We also get much information on Hitchcock's relations with Selznick, Hecht, and other big movie names, as well as on the actual techniques behind such classic scenes as the shower scene in **Psycho** and the monument chase in **North by Northwest**.

Considering the lack of cooperation from the family, the wealth of detail in the book is incredible. By interviews, researching memos, watching films, etc., Spoto has come up with as extensive a biography as we could reasonably expect.

Only three other quibbles: (1) Spoto, like most critics, seems to underrate the 1953 film, **I Confess**, which I think was first-rate Hitchcock. (2) He consistently uses the word "precipitous" when he means "precipitate." So do most people, I guess, except for Edwin Newman. (3) He implies that Helen Simpson was still alive in 1948 when Hitchcock filmed her novel, **Under Capricorn**. She had been killed in a bombing raid in London during World War II.

Not a bad record for a thick, interesting book crammed with information and opinions. This biography is enjoyable to read, and it will make you want to see all the Hitchcock films again.

A recent paperback original from Fawcett Gold Medal, William Appel's **Watcher Within** (1983), is a modern-day **Rear Window**. The hero is an agoraphobic writer, virtually house-confined, whose window overlooks a Hebrew Institute. There, he sees a deranged Talmudic scholar lure prostitutes to their eventual deaths on Sabbaths when the building is otherwise empty. While I can't see a younger Jimmie Stewart playing the hero, there are characters in this book which seem based on the late Grace Kelly and Thelma Ritter in the film **Rear Window**. **The Watcher Within** is ultimately suspenseful as it resolves the question of whether the hero, faced with murder and danger to the woman he loves, can bring himself to leave his home. Yet it lacks much of the impact of the Cornell Woolrich novelet which Hitchcock used so well in 1955.

If Hitchcock is associated with mystery films, there are two mystery radio programs that are indelibly etched in my mind's ear: **Suspense** and **The Adventures of Ellery Queen**. I was lucky enough to hear most of the latter when they were aired after 1943 (the series began in 1939). Though he never heard an Ellery Queen broadcast "live," that preeminent Queenian scholar, Francis M. "Mike" Nevins, has written as comprehensive and fascinating a book about the series as we could wish. Helped by his collaborator, Ray Stanich, who was able to provide factual information that deserves not to be buried, Nevins has added o to the scholarship he began with his Edgar-winning 1974 book, **Royal Bloodline: Ellery Queen, Author and Detective**. In 109 paperbound pages, he gives a considerable amount of information. First, there are biographies of Dannay and Lee which, despite all that has been written in the past, seem to be the first things written about their lives. How

Nevins achieved the quality of freshness there is a small miracle. Then, there is a complete history of the long-lasting radio series, with details about the plots and the actors, directors, producers, and writers (including Anthony Boucher) involved. There are a couple of pages of pictures and, finally, a chronological listing of virtually all the shows from June 18, 1939, to May 20, 1948!

The book is replete with intelligent speculation wherever precise information is unavailable. The relationship between the radio shows and the Queen short stories is described. Information is provided regarding where a few of the radio scripts can be read--e.g., in EQMM or anthologies. Ah, for an enterprising publisher to reprint these scripts as Doubleday has recently done for John Dickson Carr.

I've kept you in suspense long enough. The book to which I am referring is **The Sound of Detection: Ellery Queen's Adventures in Radio**, and it is available for $6.95 postpaid from Brownstone Books at 1711 Clifty Drive, Madison, IN 47250.

NOTES ON RECENT VIEWING

The 1982 movie, **Deathtrap**, based on Ira Levin's long-running play, works because some of surprising plot gimmicks and the performances of a small but excellent cast: Michael Caine, Christopher Reeve, Dyan Cannon, Irene Worth, and Henry Jones. Director Sidney Lumet has opened the play up a bit for the movie medium, but it is essentially is a filmed stage play. There are two changes, one minor and one major. The locale has been shifted from Connecticut to Long Island for unfathomable reasons. More important, the ending has been changed--and weakened.

The original version is available in a Penguin reprint at $4.95, and I recommend it if you suffer from what Levin calls "Thrilleritis Malignis." It's a disease that makes people want to write (and see or read) plays like **Angel St., Witness for the Prosecution, Sleuth,** and **Deathtrap.**

Deanna Durbin movies, for reasons probably unconnected with their quality, keep appearing on public television in the New York area. **Lady on a Train** is based on a Leslie Charteris story and in this 1945 B.C. (Before Christie's Mrs. McGillicuddy) film Durbin sees a murder committed from a train nearing Grand Central Station. When the police won't believe her, she turns to her favorite mystery writer, Wayne Morgan (a look-alike for the young Charteris, as played by actor David Bruce). The plot is far-fetched, but the movie is rescued by a great supporting cast, including Ralph Bellamy, Dan Duryea, Elisabeth Petterson, Edward Everett Horton, Allen Jenkins, and Patricia Morrison. It's more interesting than Durbin's musicals, but not quite up to **Christmas Holiday**, which was based on a Somerset Maugham novel. That movie, which has Gene Kelly, Gale Sondergaard, and Richard Whorf in the cast, is about a murder, though it is not strictly a mystery story. It is most notable for its New Orleans atmosphere and Durbin's rendition of that great Frank Loesser song, "Spring Will Be a Little Late This Year."

DEATH OF A MYSTERY WRITER

1. **Ross Macdonald** at age 67 in Santa Barbara, California, on July 11, 1983. Born Kenneth Millar in Los Gatos, California, he spent much of his childhood in Ontario, Canada, where he met and married

Margaret Sturm, who, as Margaret Millar, is a famous mystery writer in her own right. Her early success encouraged him to write his first mystery, **The Dark Tunnel** (1944).

As Ross Macdonald (he gave up writing under his own name to avoid confusion with his wife, and then later gave up writing as John Ross Macdonald to avoid confusion with John D. MacDonald) he is best known for his series featuring private detective Lew Archer. His books received considerable critical acclaim, and it was said that he had "lifted the modern detective novel to the level of literature." His interest in ecology was apparent in many of his books, especially his last, **The Blue Hammer** (1976), which begins on a California beach after an oil spill.

2. **Jonathan Latimer** at age 76 in La Jolla, California, on June 23, 1983. A native of Chicago, Latimer began writing in 1929 as a crime reporter with the Chicago **Herald-Examiner.** He began a popular series of mysteries about a hard-drinking Chicago private eye, Bill Crane, with **Murder in the Madhouse** (1935) and wrote four other Crane novels as well as five non-series books, one as by Peter Coffin. From 1960 to 1965 he wrote scripts for the **Perry Mason** TV series.

3. **Geoffrey Bocca** at age 59 in London on July 7, 1983. Better known as a novelist and writer of non-fiction about British royalty, Bocca wrote one mystery, **Nadine** (1974), about murder at the Cannes Film Festival.

4. **Lee Head** at age 52 in Sante Fe, New Mexico, on August 13, 1983. She wrote two mysteries--**The Terrarium** and **Crystal Clear Case**--but was better known for her Westerns, especially **Horizon** (1981), which won the Golden Spur Award of the Western Writers of America.

REEL MURDERS
MOVIE REVIEWS by Walter Albert

HOOKED ON MOVIES:
This Junkie Programs Life Around Movie Schedules and TV Guide
(with apologies to Diana Prince, Knight-News-Tribune)

It's all my parents' fault. My father would sometimes drink beer and my mother, like any good Southern Baptist, didn't like that a bit, but my parents didn't have enough money to develop any real time-consuming vices. I wish they had. Maybe if I had had a really bad example in my childhood of the awful consequences of the uncontrolled indulging in a major vice, I might have turned out differently.

They tried, of course, to teach me the proper virtues of restraint and self-control. My first conscious awareness of their attempt to rein me in is associated with **Bride of Frankenstein.** I had seen the trailer announcing the imminent scheduling of the horrific sequel to **Frankenstein.** Almost fifty years later, I can still remember vividly two isolated sequences from the film: there's a small room with actors speaking intensely and fearfully, and I can still savor that delicious feeling of enclosure and entrapment; and the Monster, Karloff in all his awesome, fearful, gripping majesty, lurches through a studio forest, bare trees stripped of all their protection and sullen rocks punctuating the skeletal landscape. That night, I began to re-run the trailer in my dreams. Only, I wasn't crouching safely in my seat, at some distance from the screen; I was in the nightmare landscape, tracked by the relentless monster, and, finally, locked inside that tiny room, listening with bated breath, waiting for the door to cave in and for a sudden, awful irruption into my little world. Needless to say, I was not allowed to see the film.

The second restraint kept me from seeing an early forties re-release of **King Kong.** The theatre entrance was partially covered with a papier-mache wall decorated with stills from the film. I was told that the film was too "exciting" and too "frightening" for me. I suspect that it was a film that my mother herself did not want to see and had manufactured an excuse to keep me from it. But the memory is out of context, and all that I associate with it is the prohibition and the theatre marquee and my disappointment. It wasn't long before I would say that I was going to the library and detour to the Roxy that showed double-features of B films and thirties films that still had some box-office life in them. By then, I had sunk to the depths. The Roxy was the cheapest and dirtiest movie in town. It was at the lower end of Main Street, where the winos, like latter-day Karloffs, lurched along the sidewalk, clutching paper bags from which they would drink furtively in recessed doorways. The Roxy had a tiny lobby, and the auditorium narrowed sharply as you approached the screen. I was always a bit uneasy there (my parents had done their underground work very well) but the tickets were cheap, the programs were long, and I was completely isolated from what guardians (parents, teachers, prissy but well-meaning friends) thought was a sordid milieu that would finally destroy. Perhaps they were right. Decades of movie going (often seeing as many as three to five films a week, and almost never fewer than two) have to do something to an impressionable mind. And when television came along with its array of bonbons for a Peter Pan with an insatiable sweet tooth, the count rose sharply.

Oh, there were the good years when I was pretending to be a dutiful graduate student, and then a dutiful husband and junior faculty member. I would sit with sweaty palms in almost empty movie palaces at afternoon showings (one of the fringe benefits of university teaching is that you don't punch a time clock), occasionally casting furtive glances about me to make sure that some other university junkie-type wasn't sitting close enough in the humid gloom to identify me to authorities waiting to cart me off to an isolation ward where I would be forced to go "cold turkey" until I was cured of the habit. But these were the years of the early Hammer films and the intrusion of mind-expanding color into the dark, austere confines of the classic horror films. I plunged like a lover newly smitten into the arms of this seductive medium, suddenly confronted with the revelation of what I must always secretly have known: film-going is not only an addiction, a habit that finally becomes as compulsive as the most addictive drug, it is an affair with the most demanding of mistresses, satisfied with nothing less than total submission to her infinite charms. Somehow, I flourished in my academic career, and children came along to give us a family of ideal size and composition, but there was always that other life and a sometimes feverish distraction that did not go unnoticed by my legal family.

There was a time in the mid- and late-seventies when there was a happy wedding of my academic and film life. The university began to encourage film studies and I was able to teach an occasional course and was even, for one improbable year, director of the Film Studies program. But the professionals soon came in, young Ph.D.s trained in film history, and I abandoned my course on vampires in film and reduced my teaching to an occasional course on French films which, with a wily deviousness I have developed in years of vice-ridden overindulgence, I advertised as covering the period from 1930 to 1960 but for which I scheduled so many films from my favorite period (the thirties) that I was able--on the flimsiest of excuses--to cover the post-World-War-II era with only four films. So far I have gotten away with it, but I am still waiting for the men in the white coats (from Western Psychiatric Institute) to break in during the showing of a film and bag me and cart me off to a de-programming from which I would emerge with a revised syllabus and some canned, organized lectures in which there is nary a hint of passion or eccentricity.

The crisis came this fall at the first meeting of the Film Studies central committee, now dominated by earnest, capable English Department types, untenured mostly, and fearful of what the next department review will bring. We were discussing some course submissions and one of the most earnest of that earnest crew, a bright, well-qualified young woman, spoke up: "He doesn't understand that it's all a question of shots; why this (and she shuddered, expressing a revulsion that brushed me with its dark, deadly wings) ... person doesn't have any idea of what film really is...." Shocked, we looked again, more closely, at the course description. She's right, I thought, this person doesn't know what it's all about ... and this person could be ME!

I went away from that meeting resolved to be a better person. Pleading other business, I stopped going out to the movies; I found that I could no longer remember TV film schedules without poring over them endlessly, my lips moving as I silently read and tried to assimilate; and I welcomed the take-over of the TV room by my children. I'm really free of this addiction, I thought to myself. I stopped watching "Sneak Previews" and hating the ill-informed new team; I didn't read the film guid in **The New Yorker** on my way to the intermittent Kael columns; I believed every negative review I read (thus justifying my non-attendance), and when I had the TV control I hopped about from channel to channel, sampling and rejecting, until I finally stopped sampling.

It was over. I had finally broken the ties that bind. I could now returned to the book on Giraudoux abandoned ten years ago in mid-sabbatical when I had my mid-life crisis. I would never again be a movie junkie.

Two nights ago, after a month of relative abstinence, in a burst of unaccustomed generosity, I offered to take my wife to see **Gandhi** at a neighborhood theater. We arrived early for the one showing, she fortified with a **New York Times** crossword puzzle, I with a borrowed copy of **The Absolute Sound**, an underground magazine for audiophile and analogue recording junkies. The theatre began to fill and, as the lights lowered portentiously, I sat in my favorite aisle seat, chewing on a surviving fingernail, waiting for the jolt that was sure to come. Then, for three hours, I underwent a slow death; and when the film ended, just before midnight, I uncurled and followed my wife into the night, hating the turgid film I had just seen, hating the Academy for giving Richard Attenborough an undeserved award and remembering as my only real moment of pleasure the assassination (which we saw two times from different perspectives) which signaled the end of the film.

Yes, it was really over. If I couldn't like such a deserving film as **Gandhi**, I was a perverse, uncaring, self-indulgent dilettante and I was right to refuse my wilful affection to an indiscriminate habit. That seemed to be a good moment, a moment in which all things were clear to me, and I was finally going to be a better person.

Last night the kids were out, my wife was working at the computer, the cats were sleeping somewhere, and the dog was entertaining his fleas on the windowseat. I had spent a pleasant day socializing with French types at the fall meeting of the American Association of Teachers of French, was looking forward to grading papers and preparing a class on Sunday, and had nothing pressing to do that evening. I wandered restlessly into the TV room and plopped down on the sofa. Perhaps I would spend the evening staring at the ceiling and thinking about constructive things to do with my life now that the film demon had been exorcised.

My hand fell to the floor and landed on the TV control. Almost instinctively my fingers wrapped themselves around it and raised it to eye-level. (This can't be happening to me, I thought desperately, but it was, and there was nothing I could do to stop what happened next.) An image came onto the screen. Richard Burton, looking like a zombie in the last stages of addiction, was wandering through an African setting while an incessant, exotic score propelled him and me along a crowded street. (This can't be happening to me. I am not watching this film.) It was **The Exorcist II** ("The Heretic") that I had seen recently on commercial TV before I had cleansed myself of the impure spirit. But the images began to take hold. The movie has many of the qualities of a dream, dense with unresolved but significant images, and it moves with all the slow, maddening, necessary impulse of a dream that surely must end badly. Plump-cheeked, but somehow sympathetic and appealing Linda Blair was drawn back toward the Georgetown house of **The Exorcist**, while Dr. Louise Fletcher, with her monotonous voice and off-center acting (she never seems to connect with the other actors or with the situation), dumped her children with a babysitter and headed off to Washington with Kitty Winn. (I don't like this. I am not going to watch this. I have already seen it. I do not want to watch this again.) A spectacular crash outside the Georgetown house leaves the taxidriver dead with the broken steering wheel driven into his neck and the violence and anxiety mount to almost unbearable levels .... And I watch the film.

At midnight, **Smithereens** follows, with its touching performance by Susan Berman as a young New Yorker conned by herself and her musician lover into thinking that she will be able to run away and finding that she is never going to be able to run away from herself or the back streets of the city. The movie ends as she turns toward a driver who is trying to pick her up. She refuses twice and the third time she may accept ... and the movie ends .... The young June Lockhart is being reassured by Sara Haden on another channel that she surely is not a werewolf, and then I settle in with Rip Torn at a Vegas blackjack table where he loses a bundle to dealer Ken Wahl. The film is about half over and Bette Midler is prowling about in a mobile home and I know that I am watching a recent box office bomb, **Jinxed**, that I find I am enjoying for Midler's funny, sharp performance and Rip Torn's memorable extended sequence as a corpse Wahl and Midler are trying to dispose of. Jack Elam turns up as a lascivious desert rat, and the film has some of the cockeyed, offkey humor of **Smithereens**.

It was 3 a.m., and I had watched three films that had gone nowhere at the box office. Two of them were substantially budgeted productions that were blasted by the critics and ignored by the public, and one was a low-budget film that was not widely reviewed and was certainly also ignored by the audience. And I had enjoyed all three of them.

Today is a bright, cool, late-October Sunday. I will be leaving in about thirty minutes for a forty-five minute drive to a suburban theater to see **Brainstorm** in a theater that is equipped with Dolby Stereo equipment. And I will have time before I leave to line up my TV viewing for the week. There is a stack of **New Yorkers** with unread Kael reviews, a Reader's's Subscription promotion with Kael's **5000 Nights at the Movies** as one of its lures, the **New York Times** entertainment section is on the front-hall table, Channel 53 is into a W.C. Fields festival, and I think that I may have enough time before class tomorrow to get most of the papers graded. It's about time I worked through some of the back issues of **Cinefantastique, Film Comment, American Cinematographer, Gore Creatures**, and Steinbrunner and Godfrey columns in EQMM and TAD. And didn't I pick up the latest **Alfred Hitchcock Magazine** with some film notes? By the way, there is a collectibles' fair in Mellon Park and there are usually some film books and ....

I have another sabbatical coming up and I think I will try to get down to work on my book on James Whale.

VERDICTS
Book Reviews

Diana Cooper-Clark. **Designs of Darkness: Interviews with Detective Novelists.** Bowling Green State University Popular Press, 1983, 229 pp., $19.95 cloth, $9.95 paper.

    It is undeniably a Bad Thing to review a book which you have not read, and it is an Even Worse Thing when such a review is hostile, but I just can't help myself. There is a certain kind of work which rubs my hackles the wrong way, and this book epitomizes that class.
    I hardly know where to start, there is so much about which to complain. Probably I should begin with what I regard as the all pervading fault of the work, and that is the author's narcissistic pretentiousness. The tone is set by the very first sentence of the introduction--"There was a time when I was a snob"--said in the same spirit as Reagan's occasional admissions than he was once a Democrat, and with the same glee as the evangelical bible-pounders confess to having once been sinners. In all three instances the admission is made for the prime purpose of eliciting congratulations for having overcome the awful shortcoming. In Cooper-Clark's case, however, she immediately demonstrates that, while she may have convinced herself that she is no longer a snob because she now reads mysteries, she is the quintessential snob of the precious, don't-you-think-highly-of-me-because I'm-so-erudite school of snobbery. Actually, one does not have to wait until the first page for the first hints of what is to come--the three quotations following the acknowledgements page (from Ionesco, Eliot, and St. Luke) serve no purpose other than to demonstrate how well-read Cooper-Clark is. The name dropping begins in earnest on the second page of the introduction--on the first page she is uncharacteristically subdued, managing only one superfluous quotation from a Wilfrid Sheed novel. On page two we encounter the names of William Goldman, Jacques Barzun ("Jacques Barzun reassured me ..."), Phillip Guedalla, Q.D. Leavis, George Eliot, T.S. Eliot, William Faulkner, Jorges Luis Borges, William Burroughs, Donald Barthelme, W.H. Auden, W.B. Yeats, George Bernard Shaw, Heinrich Boll, Ellen Glasgow, Edith Wharton, Arthur Miller, Bertrand Russell, Joseph Wood Krutch, Northrop Frye, Geoffrey Hartman, and Margaret Atwood. These self-congratulatory name-droppings, which serve no other purpose than to show off Cooper-Clark's all-encompassing knowledge of literary types, are interspersed at regular intervals by recondite bits of esoteric knowledge designed to convince us that here is a person that Lord Peter Wimsey himself or even Philo Vance would have trouble keeping up with: "Perhaps the Ife tribe in Africa is on to something. They

have no word for art. Their word for art is life." Cooper-Clark immediately knocks in the head any idea that we might have that she reads mysteries merely for their entertainment value:

> Mostly, my reading raised many questions. My introduction can only hope to reflect part of the motion of my mind rather than produce the book length answers the questions surely deserve. What has the term "greatness" come to mean in our time? Why is our certifiably great literature inaccessible to many contemporary readers? Can great literature be read by most people or is it by definition exclusive. How is it that illiterate (in both the connotative and denotative. sense) people in the past were fully conversant with the House of Atreus yet university students today can sometimes hardly pronouce [sic] their names, much less remember them....

Etc., etc, **ad nauseum.** [Please forgive the Latin; it must be the company I've been keeping.]

Cooper-Clark takes a name-dropping breather on page three, mentioning only Spenser, Swinburne, and--just so we'll know that her knowledge is truly catholic--Toni Morrison, but she's back in form on page four, throwing out Roland Barthes, Thomas Hardy, Dostoevski, Robertson Davies, Shakespeare, Euripedes, Robert Browning, Camus, James Dickey, Walker Percy, John Cheever, William Faulkner, Alain Robbe-Grillet, Nathalie Sarraute, Michel Butor, Cynthia Grenier, Doris Lessing, and Andrew Lang, as well as mentioning **Oedipus Rex, The Aeneid,** The Arabian Nights, and Chaucer's tales in passing. Another breather on page five, made necessary by the fact that she uses most of the page for a long quotation from Hillary Waugh. Even so, she manages to mention Dickens, Francis Meres, Isaac Bashevis Singer, and Flannery O'Conner. Then it's off again on page six, with Thackeray, Carlyle, Eliot, Meredith, Stendhal, Tolstoy, Mark Twain, Julio Cortazar, Northrop Frye, and Zahava K. Dorinson dropping around us like hailstones while Cooper-Clark reinforces her image of literary omniscience with sentences such as this: "Perhaps we should accept the conventions of the detective story just as we accept the conventions of other forms--the sonnet, the dramatic monologue, masques, the epic poem, Horatian or Juvenalian satire, Aristotelian or Elizabethan tragedy." This listing of "other forms," once again, serves no purpose other than to show off Cooper-Clarks erudition.

Also serving no purpose would be further listings of Cooper-Clarks name-dropping excesses. Would that that were her only fault. In fact, however, she is the kind of writer who would try to embue a shopping list with cosmic significance. Consequently, clear, concise, and straightforward prose is quite beyond her. Here is one of her simpler, least pretentious paragraphs [honest!]:

> Criticism in the twentieth century, most particularly the New Criticism, was basically a revolt against the Aristotelian and the Western humanistic traditions. This critical spirit found an analogue in the influence of the East. We were exposed to a new way of seeing. We were urged to move beyond our formulas for exegetics, our rational modes of thought, our linear perception of the world, into a world that redefined and even rejected coherence. The revolt took its form in a rejection of

"prose" in favor of "poetry," a rejection of linear plots and chronological time in favor of time that is telescoped, simultaneous and circular, a rejection of the closed ending, the resolution, in favor of an open or on-going non-conclusion, a rejection of books and even sentences with beginnings, middles and ends, a rejection of the well-made play or novel (**la piece bien faite**), and a rejection of the conscious, rational world in favor of the subconscious, the irrational. Within this critical sensibility, the detective novel would seem archaic and hopelessly minor.

If your taste runs to bullshit, you'll find it here in abundance.
So how does our hyphenated cutie end this orgy of self-congratulation? Just as you might expect:

> I started as an uninformed snob. Where am I now? I must confess that I am not a "buff." But I am firmly committed to the excellence of the writers in this book. Among the past masters I particularly enjoy G.K. Chesterton, Raymond Chandler, Josephine Tey and Robert van Gulik. I find books that are not strictly within the genre, such as J.B. Priestley's **The Shapes of Sleep**, C.P. Snow's **A Coat of Varnish** and the writing of Friedrich Durrenmatt, utterly intriguing. There are others that I have read and doubtless many meritorious that I have not read or perhaps have read but do not particularly like. But the point is that I have learned much and enjoyed fully.

Hrrumph! The point, I would say, is that Ms. CooperhyphenClark has clearly disassociated herself from us garden-variety mystery fans and has shown that it is possible for a person of impeccable literary taste and general over-all brilliance--Ms. Cooper-Clark, for example--to enjoy certain practitioners of the mystery writer's art, so long as they have qualities which raise them above the common herd of plebian hacks--among whom, I venture to guess, she would number most of the authors you and I would count among the greats in the field. In other words, Cooper-Clark started as an uninformed snob and she ends as one. I have no doubt that she would look down her superior, patrician nose at **TMF** and its contributors and their enthusiasms as pandering to the tastes of the great unwashed. Well, all I've got to say is, Come the revolution ....
  But, no, that's not all I have to say. Cooper-Clark belongs to the Barbara Walters school of interviewers, in that her principal aim is to ask questions which will elevate her in the eyes of her readers or watchers rather than questions which will elicit a significant response from the person being interviewed. Here, for example, is one of the "questions" Cooper-Clark asked of P.D. James:

> Morality is a central part of classical British literature in general. The detective novel is a part of this British tradition. In your work, one aspect of this mainstream is the emphasis on upright moral behavior. E.M.W. Tillyard, in **The Elizabethan World Picture**, has said that English literature as a whole has spoken an idiom permeated with Christian dogma. In this respect the detective can perhaps be seen as the archetypal Moses

or Joshua who instructs or guides a bewildered people and brings them to justice. Dalgleish in **Death of an Expert Witness** does not come down from a mountain but he does come down from a helicopter. The question of "justice" is debated beautifully in that book between Dr. Kerrison's daughter, Eleanor, and Dalgleish, when she questions him as to the validity of imprisoning the murderer when he cannot alter the crime, and then wonders whether the murderer who kills an old and dying man who has only one week to live should go to jail. Do you see this aspect of morality as an extension of concerns that are central to the British novel?

And here's a "question" she asked of Jean Stubbs:

> There is also a darker side to women. In the eighteenth and nineteenth centuries, the fashionable went as spectators to murder trials, and many were women. These genteel women were fascinated by cold blooded murder. This is reflected in the novels of the time and the trials in **Dear Laura**, **The Case of Kitty Ogilvie** and **My Grand Enemy**. In Julie Kavanagh's **Sybil's Second Love**, Mrs. Mush says, "I dearly like a murder. Of course, I do not wish for murders but when there is one, why I like it. It is human nature." Thomas Carlyle's sister, Jane, wrote in her journal about Palmer, the physician-poisoner, whose case was a sensation of the day: "From first to last he has preserved the most wonderful coolness, forcing a certain admiration from one, murderer tho' he be!" How do you account for this dichotomy; on the one hand, the surface gentility and on the other hand, the clear fascination with 'horrible murder.'[sic]

As you might guess, the answer Stubbs gives is only about half the length of the so-called "question." Indeed, one gets, in reading through these "interviews," the impression that, like her role model, Barbara Walters, Cooper-Clark waits impatiently for her subject to finish speaking so that the focus of attention will revert to her and she can ask another of her interminably long questions.

My view is that the interviewer's purpose should be to elicit information from the interviewee. Cooper-Clark's view seems to be that interviewees are necessary evils, put on earth for the prime purpose of giving interviewers someone off whom to bounce their brilliant questions. Their answers don't matter; it's the question that counts.

A while back--I can't be more precise because my back issues are in temporary storage--I picked up a newly-arrived copy of **TAD** and began reading an interview article. I didn't get very far, because the interviewer approached her task in exactly the same way that Cooper-Clark approaches her's. In fact, I'd be willing to bet that the article was written by Cooper-Clark--surely there can't be two such equine anuses running loose. I threw the magazine down in disgust--something I have never done before or since with **TAD**--and I never read another word in that issue.

From the preceding tirade, which I draw to a premature close (I could go on all evening without repeating myself), you are probably expecting me to advise you to steer clear of this book. Well, I'm not going to. Cooper-Clark has interviewed thirteen mystery writers--P.D.

James, Jean Stubbs, Peter Lovesey, Margaret Millar, Ross Macdonald, Howard Engel, Ruth Rendell, Janwillem van de Wetering, Patricia Highsmith, Julian Symons, Amanda Cross, Anne Perry, and Dick Francis--and, despite herself, she does allow them to get an occasional word in edgewise. Of course, you have to wade through incredible amounts of Cooper-Clark claptrap to get to these morsels, but I'm looking forward to reading several of these interviews just as soon as I get my strength back. One happy circumstance: Cooper-Clark's contribution to the book seems to have been confined to contriving all those wonderful questions, so it is conceivable that the responses of the interviews are substantially as they were given. I quote from the "Acknowledgements" page: "I would like to thank the secretarial services at York University for the excellent job they did in transcribing the interviews from the tapes and then typing the book." Thank God for small favors.

Two last complaints. First, all the interviewees except one consented to have their photos taken by Cooper-Clark's husband, Trevor Clark (who is evidently having to struggle through life without a hyphen to call his own). Evidently Cooper-Clark and the hyphenless Trevor made the mistake of letting Amanda Cross see some of the other photos and she wisely chose to remain a blank page. The kindest thing I can think of to say about the dozen photos that appear in the back--and the shot of Cooper-Clark herself which adorns the back cover--is that they are all in focus. And finally, I must confess that my opinion of Canadian higher education has been dealt a crippling blow by this book, on the back cover of which I read that "Diana Cooper-Clark teaches at York University, Toronto [sic] in the Atkinson College English and Humanities Departments." I know that Americans, even some American English professors, haven't the foggiest notion of how commas are used, but until Cooper-Clark's painful prose disabused me of the idea, I thought the Canadians were still privy to the secret. (Guy M. Townsend)

Stephen Brett. **Some Die Hard.** Manor, 1979.

Any book that refers on its cover to "a hip young private eye" has got off to a bad start. This one scarcely improves as Rock Dugan (Rock, for goodness sake!) is taken on as bodyguard to a wealthy man. The one bright spot is a neatly posed impossible crime, as Dugan's employer is stabbed to death in a light plane of which he is the only occupant. However, the heavy clouds have descended again by the time a rather fatuous solution (early twenties type) is provided. Utterly forgettable. (Bob Adey)

Stephen Robinett. **The Man Responsible.** Ace, 1978.

Set in the twenty-first century, this is one of the happiest mixtures of science fiction and detective fiction that I've come across. Harry Penny is a lawyer retained to investigate the dealings of Silver River Development, a multinational land venture. The detective problem is all to do with whether a vast corporate fiddle is being perpetrated, and, if so, by whom; the science fiction is handled in a low key, matter-of-fact style that carries absolute conviction. Surely this world of advanced computer technology and holographic projections is what the citizens of 2000 + will face. The writing is excellent and posed no problems to that most untechnical of people--me. Strongly recommended. (Bob Adey)

Michael Allen. **Spence in Petal Park.** Constable, 1977.

This is the first of three (so far) police procedurals about Superintendent Ben Spence. In this one he investigates the murder of apparently well-to-do Roger Parnell and uncovers a veritable sewer of cross currents. What makes this a very good book indeed is the flesh and blood the author puts into all his characters, and the psychology he applies. And detection there certainly is, too, with a fair conclusion to the case. All in all one of the finds of the year and easily enough to start me looking for the other two Spence investigations. (Bob Adey)

Michelle Collins. **Murder at Willow Run.** Zebra, 1979.

This is one of a series of gimmick paperback originals with a sealed section containing the solution chapter and unhelpful picture clues at intervals throughout the book. Like most such gimmicks, it's not great literature. In fact, the prose is as bad as anything I've read (post war) in a long time, and fatuous examples fill the pages--"from the consensus of gestures---"; "She gathered her long hair and bunched it on top of her head, ventilating the back of her neck"; "Winter was scheduled to arrive any time now." At best, odd use of words must be the indictment.
As for the plot (including a locked-room murder with a time-worn solution), no original thought intrudes. (Bob Adey)

Fred Zackel. **Cocaine and Blue Eyes.** Coward, 1978.

Long, humourless novel about p.i. Michael Brennan and his search for Dani with the startling blue eyes. It starts promisingly enough, but I became bored with the characters and the toings and froings, and I frankly couldn't for the life of me see why Brennan didn't clear out long before with his dead client's money. I'm afraid that I would have done. Disappointing, but I'll probably still read his second book. (Bob Adey)

Judith Worrell. **Sting of the Bee.** Tower, 1982, $2.50.

Given the fact that the women's movement has--at least in the lip-service and on-the-surface departments--changed some of the roles women play in our society, and given the fact that crime writers haven't been at all slow to seize this new potential for book sales, it was probably only a matter of time until we got a book about an amateur detective who is a former nun. Maura Cleary, hero of Judith Worrell's **Sting of the Bee**, is the first of that ilk whom I've met. Having moved from New York City to Maine seeking peace, bucolic surroundings, and a means of serving humanity outside the Order of Holy Love, Maura quickly discovers that in her new small-town home, provincialism, gossip, and murder all threaten her privacy, her peace of mind, and even, perhaps, her life.
When an acquaintance is stung to death by bees, Maura undertakes to solve the mystery in order to protect some of the clients of her social welfare agency and her long-time, though prickly, friend,

Sonia, visiting at the time of the murder. Clearly, the victim, Sonia, and Maura herself are meant to be studies in contrast, and to a fair degree the aim is fulfilled. Maura's tentative love affair is handled with restraint. There are also touches of humor, often successful, usually promising, and Worrell does allow some touching (and fairly well controlled) insights to the difficulty of Maura's transition into life wholly "in the world."

If Worrell can avoid a serious case of the cutes in future outings as she sometimes fails to do here (Maura's agency is called Community Life Improvement Program: CLIP, for instance), she could turn promise into fulfillment. (Jane S. Bakerman)

Jane Langton. **Natural Enemy.** Ticknor & Fields, 1982, 282 pp.

In Jane Langton's new mystery about Homer Kelly, her series detective, and Mary, his delightful wife, several other familiar faces from earlier works (**The Transcendental Murder, Dark Nantucket Noon,** and **The Memorial Hall Murder**) also appear in minor roles, but the true center of the book is the Kellys' college-bound nephew, John Hand, whose temporary job involves him in murder--and love. Budget cutbacks have done away with John's usual summer employment, doing maintenance work for Lincoln, Massachusetts, and so he takes a job as man-of-all-work for Barbara and Virginia Heron, young women whose father is murdered almost simultaneously with John's arrival on the scene. John is not a suspect, but he is very much involved in the final imposition of justice upon one of Langton's most selfish, scheming, unappealing killers. The murderer in this inverted mystery is also a suitor for the hand of Virginia Heron, the "older woman" (she is about twenty-two or twenty-three) whom John loves, and Langton's sketch of the boy's emotions, responses, agonies, and joys is very well done indeed. It's a pleasure to accompany John Hand during his initiation into manhood.

Homer and Mary Kelly are on the spot because they are staying in Concord to oversee John's youngest sibling, Benny, while the Hand parents and other children are off on an extended trip. Precocious Benny belongs well and truly in the company of kids like Red Chief; he's brilliant, mischievous, annoying, and funny, perhaps not a surprising offspring for the Kelly Hand clan to produce, and one of his main activities is "wearing Homer down," as the scholar-detective is quick to confess. Benny's Benniness is interfering with Homer's work--and making Homer feel old, decayed, and helpless.

The Benny element in the novel is fun, but, as usual, one of the chief delights is the "outside interest" apparatus with which Langton customarily embellishes her books. In this case, it's spiders. John is a budding entomologist, planning to specialize in spiders. His small collection is sound; his modes of observation are worthy, and his summer-long study of a barn spider frames the mystery, lends interest, and serves the symbol structure well. Like John, the spider survives trouble and growth, and the reader comes to realize that she's as pretty and as interesting as John early on declares her to be.

Once again, then, Jane Langton has created a workable mystery, enlarged her portraits of the Kellys, and produced a cast of especially intriguing supportive characters. She has also illustrated this book as she has done earlier. A woman of many talents, Langton has put them to good use here. Readers will enjoy **Natural Enemy.** (Jane S. Bakerman)

Margaret Yorke. **The Hand of Death.** St. Martin's, 1981, 218 pp.

In **The Hand of Death,** Margaret Yorke produces a strong, psychological study of several characters, most prominently the rapist-killer in this inverted mystery. He is Ronald Trimm, antiques dealer, secret porer over girlie magazines. Trim is unsavory, unattractive, and dangerous, but he is not a monster. Yorke paints a portrait too full and too detailed for that, as is almost always the case in her absorbing stories. One detail--one implied motivation for Trimm's penchant for pornography and rape--strikes a discordant note. Nancy Trimm, Ronald's business partner and wife, is another of Yorke's cold, unfeeling, calculating women, almost all of them wives who complicate their husbands' lives, sometimes destroying their spouses in the process. This kind of relationship has become a kind of theme in Yorke's work, and while it is certainly a subject of importance, it falters a bit here. Nancy is to be blamed for trapping a husband merely to satisfy society's demands for "success" in a woman's life, but Ronald is such an unattractive piece of goods, it's a little hard to blame her as much as Yorke seems to wish readers to do. And frustration, of course, is not adequate (what is?) nor really accurate motivation for rape. Much more realistic is the suppressed rage Trimm evidences very convincingly.

Much more accurate, very realistic, and touching in a very controlled way is Yorke's treatment of the reactions of one of Trimm's victims, Valerie Turner, whom he rapes. though she has guts and strength, Valerie is rendered helpless by Trimm's threats against her children, terrified because her home has been invaded, and stunned at the exploitation of her body. Her gradual return to something like normalcy (which includes coming to be of use to the police after Trimm kills an intended rape victim) is a good, useful subplot.

The initial suspect in the murder (of a lonely, feckless widow who first seduces and then spurns the luckless Trimm) is unhappy George Fortescue, who is trying to rebuild his life (chiefly by taking up jogging, it seems!) after his wife has deserted him. Known to be outraged, known to be lonely, and assumed to be frustrated, George seems a likely suspect to the locals, and circumstances conspire against him. the Fortescue and Trimm marriages are compared and contrasted neatly, and the pattern of exploitativeness (both Nancy Trimm and George Fortescue are masters at behaving selfishly toward their spouses) is itself neatly exploited by Yorke, who often uses comparison and contrast to good effect.

A group of young folk, more appealing than many teenagers Yorke has invented, complete the main cast: Trimm's employee, George's son, the daughter of the murder victim, and their cronies appear, trying to do their best in a puzzling world, in awkward situations not of their own making. Yorke allows a good deal of hope for these youngsters as well as for those adults capable of learning, growing, and changing.

Taken all in all, **The Hand of Death** is among Yorke's most satisfying mysteries; it's quite a bit more than just "a good read." (Jane S. Bakerman)

Diane Johnson. **The Shadow Knows.** Vintage Books, 1982, 254 pp.

Originally published in 1974, Diane Johnson's novel **The Shadow Knows** well deserves its currently available reprint, for it is a compelling study in suspense. It is also funny, anguished, frightening, and open-ended, a potential victim's account of the torturous period during which she waits for a crime to happen. For fans of mystery fiction, it is eminently readable as an experiment in form, achieved by the author's use of the most amateur of amateur detectives, who tells her own story, confessing her own "crimes of the human heart," analyzing her own terror, explaining her frantic, usually subjective, sometimes illogical attempts at ratiocination, and comparing her efforts to those she imagines a stern, all-knowing, all-powerful, male Famous Inspector would make. 'Her key question, perhaps even more central than the question of the identity of the threatener, is "if someone is trying to kill you, do you maybe deserve it?"

For protagonist N. Hexam, life is in serious disarray--recently divorced, she is trying to rear her four children, fend off the angry forays of her former husband and a former maid, cope with the shifting feelings of her married lover, work on a graduate degree, sustain her relationship with her housekeeper, and avoid getting murdered. Amid all these strenuous endeavors (which seem oddly but convincingly equal in importance to her) she finds the time to keep the journal which is the novel. A series of alarming events precipitate the beginning of the journal--harrassment by a "Phantom Phone-caller," vandalization of her front door, and an aborted breaking and entering. Other frightening moments occur and are recorded along with the flashbacks into N. Hexam's past which are her attempts to discover who the threatener is and if she deserves to be threatened.

The journal is a variant form of the traditional detective's traditional list of clues, suspects, and motives as well as a variation from the retrospective tone of most first person detective stories. These factors, the use of the victim as investigator, and other experiments with standard elements of mystery fiction, form a fascinating pattern overlaying the basic studies in suspense and characterization. Amazingly and satisfyingly, it all works and works with one last inversion--terrible though it is, the crime, when it ultimately takes place, relieves rather than incites the suspense and tension. (Jane S. Bakerman)

Delano Ames. **Murder, Maestro, Please.** Perennial Library, 1952.

Although the title implies a musical theme, the Puig d'Aze Music Festival has little to do with this tale of murder and detection. More central to the plot are Jane and Dagobert Brown and their array of friends/enemies. Narrated by Jane, with light humor and sarcastic understatement, it is a fine example of "ladies" fiction from earlier times. It is bland, non-threatening, cutesy, and thoroughly enjoyable if read relatively quickly and without much thought.

The main attraction is Jane and Dagobert. They are a young, charming couple who understand each other and have no need to worry about money or any of the other mundane cares of life. Jane may make caustic comments about the time Dagobert spends with a fetching young suspect, but in her heart she knows to whom he belongs. Of course, there is a problem with the young lovers (which girl will the brash American end up with?). And Jane's school friend, Naomi, is acting very odd--could the story of her carrying on an affair with Johnny Corcoran be true?

And then there's the harpsichord prodigy, Mitzi Stein (one of the few connections to the Festival), with her stories of Russian spies and concentration camps. And finally there's Kitson, the harpsichord maestro himself, in whose honor the Festival is being held. Actually, he is something of a drunk and an admitted fraud in his opinion of music.

Stir all these characters (plus a few more) and potential plot elements with a lot of night-time action and vague, cryptic remarks. The result is light fiction as practiced by Leslie Ford, Kelly Roos, and the Lockridges in their Mr. & Mrs. North books. Perhaps most surprising is that Jane and Dagobert are British rather than American. Oh, yes--there's a murder or two that occur and get solved in a classic calling-together-of-the-suspects scene. (Fred Dueren)

Delano Ames. **For Old Crime's Sake.** Perennial Library, 1959.

The last of the Dagobert and Jane Brown series shows the strain and fatigue of trying to realistically have a pair of amateur detectives solve a dozen murders in as many years. Jane, the narrator, rambles around talking to various suspects and co-travelers on a contest trip to the island of Tabarca. Dagobert refuses to be left behind, so he trails along on a motorcycle, picking up a hitchhiker for company.

One of the contest winners disappears from the boat while crossing to France, but no one ever gets too upset, so we are not sure whether there's been a murder or not. Eventually there is a corpse--after all everyone had so much to hide in their past, it was bound to happen sometime. Dagobert reveals the killer without too many explanations of how he knew.

It's not all as bad as it sounds. Somehow Jane and Dagobert still come off as a charming couple, close and loving but always at humorous odds. There's an air of irresponsible escapism that's hard to resist, as long as you're not looking too deep. (Fred Dueren)

Elizabeth Lemarchand. **Unhappy Returns.** Walker, 1983 [first published in 1977], 175 pp., $2.95.

For its new line of paperback mysteries, Walker is wisely reprinting the British authors they have previously printed in hard covers. The traditionalist will curse them somewhat for adding another line of irresistible paperbacks each month. With all the excellent selections from Dell, Perennial Library, Scribners, Vintage, and Pantheon, who would have thought there would be room for more?

Anyway, Superintendent Pollard and Inspector Toye of Scotland yard are with us again. Their problem this time is the murder of Ethel Ridd, a waspish spinster who was the housekeeper for the late Barnabus Viney, rector of Abercombe. Before she died, Ethel claimed that the rector had had a small jewelled chalice that cannot now be found among the church plate. After several false starts, Pollard's steady procedure puts him on the track of the right answer. Quiet and unobtrusive, **Unhappy Returns** is a pleasurable diversion. (Fred Dueren)

Albrecht Weber. **Das Phanomen Simmel: Zur Rezeption eines Bestseller-Authors unter Schulern und im Literaturunterricht** [The Simmel Phenomenon: The Reception of a Bestseller Author by Schoolchildren and in Literature Instruction] (Herder Taschenbuch Band 9303). Freiburg, Germany: Herderbucherei, 1977, 189 pp.

This is an academic German pedagogical examination of the work of Johannes Mario Simmel, author of long-winded thrillers such as **I**

Confess, The Cain Conspiracy, The Monte Cristo Cover-Up, and The Traitor Blitz. Weber designed and helped carry out a public opinion survey to ask questions of German gymnasium (= high school) students and teachers regarding Simmel. Some of the results were that eighty percent of all students had heard of Simmel and fifty percent had read at least one book by him, most frequently It Can't Always Be Caviar (1965). However, most teachers found Simmel unworthy to be taught in literature courses.

Although this book contains a great deal of statistical material of absolutely no criminous interest, there is also some interesting discussion of the "popular literature vs. Literature" question (in German, popular literature is usually referred to as "Trivialliteratur"). Weber argues that Simmel's work can fall into either category and that his works should be taught in schools. As an aid to teachers considering teaching Simmel, Weber handily provides plot summaries and literary interpretations of It Can't Always Be Caviar and Love Is Just a Word. It also includes a bibliography of Simmel's books through 1976 and a bibliography of secondary sources.

Although this book seems boring to the criminously interested reader (much of it is boring), the important thing about it is that it exists. Weber seems to be a long-time Simmel fan, and it is good of him to have championed the cause and provided what is in effect a book-length apologia for the respectability of a writer who is primarily known as a "krimi" author. It is also curious that it exists in Germany, where the gap between popular literature and "Literature" is wider than it is in America, where to my knowledge there has been no similar study. (Greg Goode)

S.F.X. Dean. **By Frequent Anguish**. Walker, 1982, 211 pp., $9.95.

This love-story-cum-murder-mystery tries hard to be liked, but I somehow found myself constantly off-stride with it.

I always enjoy mysteries with an academic setting, for example, but here it seems stylized (and fossilized) to an extreme: the many and varied eccentrics on the faculty, the "gung ho" students (but for what?), and, of course, the inevitable town-gown confrontation.

That's run-of-the-mill carping, though. What I found that really bothered me was the victim herself: a beautiful (and bright!) coed in love with her professor, Neil Kelly, who by necessity finds himself the detective who must solve her murder. (He, also, had just discovered that he was in love with her. No wonder the publisher calls this "A Love Story Interrupted by a Murder.")

Oddly repellent, or flying in the face of old-fashioned traditions: take your pick. In either case, it doesn't quite work. It's too sad for a love story, and it's too linear and direct (and yet not entirely fair) for a mystery.

It's greatest redeeming feature is that you can say entirely the same sorts of things, of course, about life itself. [C plus] (Steve Lewis)

James McKimmey. **Blue Mascara Tears**. Ballantine, 1965, 156 pp.

In Sam Spade, as everyone knows, we had the detective as conniving con-man; in Philip Marlowe and Lew Archer, the detective as Sir Galahad. In Mike Hammer, of course, we had the detective as one-man jury. Today we have Spenser, in the role of detective as social worker, and Bill Pronzini's nameless private eye as the winner of detective fiction's hard-luck award of the year.

As the hero of this rather obscure paperback original, Jack Cummings is a cop, not a private eye, but a cop of the lone-wolf variety,. As such, not only is he definitely part of the multi-faceted p.i. tradition above, but he also extends it into directions never quite followed by any of the others in the field.

In Jack Cummings, meet the detective as Christ figure.

The similarity is in more than the initials, and no, it is not entirely coincidental. On page 42, for example, Cummings ponders what it is that he believes in, swimming as he does "through the sea, always working never to become a part of it, because the contamination would be fatal.... Was he only fooling himself, being Christ-like within his own mind and heart, but deceiving himself...?"

Or take this conversation on page 138: "The fix is cancer. Somebody's got to cure it. Who else will, if I don't?" "They'll crucify you." "It's happened to others."

It's a tough story. the terseness of the opening chapters is reminiscent of none other than Dashiell Hammett himself, and if the dialogue and the rest of the story tails off a bit in comparison--to the level of Erle Stanley Gardner, say (which is no great disparagement, to my mind, but it had to be said)--why, that's no great surprise either. In spite of all the writers who've tried it, Hammett has seldom been equalled, and certainly not for longer stretches.

Otherwise, here's a book filled with **good**, viscerally involving scenes, and plotting that's far more than merely adequate. It also features the most beautiful hooker in the world (briefly), and for the second book in a row, another victim (the girl with the tears) who did absolutely nothing to deserve her death.

If you're a lover of hard-boiled fiction, try to find this one if you can. [A] (Steve Lewis)

Douglas Clark. **Golden Rain.** Dell/Murder Ink #47, 1982 [first published in Great Britain in 1980], 222 pp., $2.50.

Let's make it four in a row. Whatever happened to the idea that the victim should be someone hated by so many people with such good motives that it takes somebody with the little gray cells of Hercule Poirot to dig out the truth and decipher at length who really did do it?

Don't conclude from this that I'm suggesting that any of Agatha Christie's victims ever **deserved** to die. And, for all I know, some of the people who died in her books were just as young and innocent as those in the last three books, plus this one.

Mystery stories--and I suppose I'm blithering unforgivably at this point because I simply don't have any other kind of statement to make--but wouldn't you agree that mysteries somehow **are** easier to take when the victim is despicable, and faceless, and with little or no other redeeming qualities?

In **Golden Rain** the victim is the headmistress of a thriving girls' school in England, and she (as it turns out) had had everything to live for. Her death by poisoning is hardly accidental, and the local inspector's conclusion, before the facts are entirely in, is that she must have committed suicide. Her superior (who should know) feels strongly otherwise.

Eventually Superintendent Masters of Scotland Yard is called in. In the grand British tradition, a good deal of "stodgy" police work follows. There is some detection involved, but overall the story is structured and told in such a way as to make it seem deliberately designed to keep the reader on the outside of it, rather than the inside, where the gears are really turning. [C plus] (Steve Lewis)

William L. Story. **Cemeteries Are for Dying.** Doubleday, 1982, 178 pp., $10.95.

William L. Story has added another to the growing list of New England based mystery stories. **Cemeteries Are for Dying** takes place in and around Boston and begins on a gristly enough note to sustain reader interest throughout the entire tale.

Peter Swann, a man of refined tastes and abundant leisure time--thanks to the largess of the state lottery--finds himself looking for answers when a young lady of his acquaintance disappears without a trace while jogging through a supposedly deserted cemetery at night.

The trail of deduction and supposition throws Peter into direct conflict with Boston's version of the mob.

Story's characterization of Swann is well done--one suspects a certain amount of autobiographical and wishful-thinking influences--and he develops the story with equal finesse. Even though the reader knows all the lurid details from page one, we follow right along with Peter in our desire to know why.

Story has set up a character and writing style in the book that are quite polished, but he uses this refined style to describe street-touch situations in a contradictory and suspenseful manner. The device works.

The ending is the only weak point, depending as it does on the proverbial eleventh-hour rescue by the cavalry, but on the whole **Cemeteries** is a quick-paced and entertaining mystery. (Alan S. Mosier)

Ellis Peters. **The Virgin in the Ice.** William Morrow & Co., 1983, 220 pp., $11.95.

I have liked the medieval Brother Cadfael since his initial appearance in **A Morbid Taste for Bones.** In this the sixth chronicle of his adventures, something has gone astray. Gone is the atmosphere, the feeling of living in the period. Peters' prose is as dry as a parchment stored in a musty monastery. What an ecclesiastical disappointment.

The tale concerns Brother Cadfael's search for a brother and sister, lost and separated after the sack of Worcester. It is a case of ships in the night, as first one is found, only to be lost as the other returns to the fold.

I found the main characters so uninteresting that I really did not care what happened to them. The whole book moves so slowly that the reader is hard-put to even finish the novel. Unfortunately, the most interesting part of the book is the title. (Alas S. Mosier)

S.T. Haymon. **Ritual Murder.** St. Martin's Press, 1982, 237 pp., $10.95.

Back in the twelfth century, a little Christian boy was found dead and mutilated around Passover time. His last errand was to get flour from a Jewish merchant. The townspeople blamed the Jews (the typical blood-of-a-Christian-to-make-matzo canard), a pogrom ensued, the boy was sainted and buried in the cathedral after some miracle cures at his grave. Eight hundred years later, the police are called in to investigate some off-color graffitti in the cathedral. The little saint's grave is undergoing some archaeological exploration (after the paving stones collapse) and, wouldn't you know it, a chorister is found murdered and mutilated in the little saint's grave. This touches off a few acts of anti-semitism, the murder investigation, and the rest of the book.

I couldn't work up much sympathy for the investigator (the two best-drawn characters are relatively minor), consequently the middle of the book sagged. This was more than compensated for by the revelation of the murderer and the reason for the murder. I fell for the red herring.

S.T. Haymon is an English woman author with one other mystery to her credit. **Ritual Murder** makes me want to look up her first book (I believe the title is **Death of a Pregnant Virgin**) the look-out for subsequent mysteries from her pen. (Linda Toole)

Beth Gutcheon. **Still Missing.** Putnam's, 1981, 364 pp.

Americans' current demand for attention to the victims of crimes is reflected in Beth gutcheon's **Still Missing**. This book is **not** a whodunit; it is **not** an inverted mystery; but it is a crime story which compares and contrasts the efforts of a young mother and of a police detective to find the kidnapper of Alexander Selky, aged almost seven, who disappears one spring morning in the course of a two-block walk to school. It's a **very** good story.

The treatment of Al Menetti's official case is well-done, conventional police procedural material--we get a sense of the tedium of detail involved in the investigation, of the officer's commitment to the law, of his anger at the viciousness of the crime, of his frustration when he fails to solve the mystery. conventionally, we also meet his family and learn that they both resent and respect his preoccupation with his work. Also conventionally (and humanly), Mrs. Menetti, Pat, is a shade jealous of the bereaved mother's claim on Al's attention. As usual, these factors provide a useful subplot and deepen the story.

But it is Susan Selky's story which rightfully dominates the book. Gutcheon's clear, restrained prose dramatizes the pain of Susan's initial loss and the sustained agony of the year we spend with her. During that year, other losses occur; friends fall--are are driven--away; a marriage finally dies; and Susan's trust in her fellow humans is seriously eroded. Though all the signs are bad, Susan retains hope of reunion with her son and stubbornly, practically mobilizes her inner forces and her social circle to sustain the search.

Still Missing is a compelling documentation of the human cost of crime. Susan loses a special kind of adult innocence; reputations are shattered; lives are permanently disrupted. these costs, of course, do not include the price Alexander Selky plays. Strong stuff, this novel--well worth reading. (Jane S. Bakerman)

Dorothy Simpson. **Six Feet Under.** Scribner's, 1982, 192 pp.

Luke Thanet, created by Dorothy Simpson, is back again, this time abetted officially by Michael Lineham, now in uniform and preparing to marry his Louise. The conscious or subconscious efforts of Lineham's mother, bent on preventing the wedding, for one major subplot to the murder plot. the victim, dowdy, repressed Carrie Birch, has spent a lifetime in thrall to **her** demanding, possessive mother. Even a limited secret life is not enough to comfort or sustain Carrie, however, and she lives vicariously by unearthing the secrets of her neighbors. One secret proves fatal; one neighbor turns killer.

Thanet's investigation uncovers all the secrets Carrie has learned and more, and though the officer proceeds with his work with capability and dispatch, many of his thoughts are elsewhere--at home, in point of fact. The Thanets' Luke-and-child-centered home life is, he feels, threatened by Joan's restlessness and her firm desire to have a demanding, rewarding job of her own. Luke Thanet surprises himself by the vehemence of his objections, which dismay and offend Joan, and for a time tension runs high between this seemingly ideal couple. Luke, however, is a fair and thoughtful man, and the lessons in human values he learns while tracking Carrie Birch's killer see him through this bad patch. While many crime writers have explored (or exploited) this aspect of some women's lives, few have done so as honorably as Simpson does here.

Six Feet Under is interesting, smooth, polished--a good, competent job. It won't surprise you, but it will please you with its sure, quiet tone and with Simpson's steady assurance in developing her craft. (Jane S. Bakerman)

Margaret Yorke. **Devil's Work**. London: Hutchinson, 1982, 170 pp.

Quite possibly, if family members (especially husbands and wives) understood one another as folksay tells us they ought, no one would ever feel the need to write a novel. So perhaps it's just as well that we have to put up with limited understanding and downright misunderstanding in order to gain the fictional benefits such authors as Margaret Yorke are so well able to create. In **Devil's Work**, Yorke once again explores the effect of unfeeling relatives upon their more sensitive kin and once again sets that examination amid painful signs of the contemporary times. Here, as in some earlier Yorke novels, a preoccupied wife unwittingly shuts off communication with her husband; he seeks comfort elsewhere land finds both solace and menace in doing so.

The current social pattern Yorke treats with insight and gentleness is early redundancy, the forced retirement of still capable, still work-oriented employees; in the novel, as in life, the excuse is tough economic times and the underlying desire of the employer to go with a younger, sprightlier worker in hope of better profit. When Alan Parker is declared redundant, he cannot bring himself to tell his independent, brisk, chattering, somewhat insensitive wife, Daphne. Instead, he pretends to go off to the office each morning, first fruitlessly seeking a new job, later filling his days as economically as he can. Humiliated and at loose ends, Alan is heartened to find himself needed by meek, beset Louise Waring, a young widow suffering from agoraphobia, and Louise's small daughter, Tessa. For a short time, the three become a sort of happy, nurturing family; all are eased; life seems almost good--and then Tessa disappears, Alan is suspected, and the novel's pace quickens to a realistic, bittersweet resolution. It won't take mystery fans more than twenty minutes to suspect who the real culprit is, and, indeed, when the crime (which takes place well into the book) does occur, it's treated as an inverted mystery, but that doesn't matter. The interest lies in the characters' responses to the threat of death, the threat of loss, and the destruction of their normal

US POSTAL SERVICE
STATEMENT OF OWNERSHIP, MANAGEMENT AND CIRCULATION
(Required by 39 U.S.C. 3685)

PUBLICATION: The Mystery Fancier

PUBLICATION NO.: 4 2 8 5 9 0

DATE OF FILING: 31 December 198_

FREQUENCY OF ISSUE: Bi-monthly

NO. OF ISSUES PUBLISHED ANNUALLY: 6

ANNUAL SUBSCRIPTION PRICE: $12.00

COMPLETE MAILING ADDRESS OF KNOWN OFFICE OF PUBLICATION *(Street, City, County, State and ZIP Code) (Not printers)*

Guy M. Townsend, 1711 Clifty Dr., Madison, IN 47250 (Jefferson County)

COMPLETE MAILING ADDRESS OF THE HEADQUARTERS OR GENERAL BUSINESS OFFICES OF THE PUBLISHERS *(Not printers)*

Same

FULL NAMES AND COMPLETE MAILING ADDRESS OF PUBLISHER, EDITOR, AND MANAGING EDITOR *(This item MUST NOT be blank)*

PUBLISHER *(Name and Complete Mailing Address)*: Same

EDITOR *(Name and Complete Mailing Address)*: Same

MANAGING EDITOR *(Name and Complete Mailing Address)*: Same

OWNER (If owned by a corporation, its name and address must be stated and also immediately thereunder the names and addresses of stockowners owning or holding 1 percent or more of total amount of stock. If not owned by a corporation, the names and addresses of the individual owners must be given. If owned by a partnership or other unincorporated firm, its name and address, as well as that of each individual must be given. If the publication is published by a nonprofit organization, its name and address must be stated.) (Item must be completed.)

FULL NAME	COMPLETE MAILING ADDRESS
Guy M. Townsend (sole owner)	1711 Clifty Dr., Madison, IN 47250

KNOWN BONDHOLDERS, MORTGAGEES, AND OTHER SECURITY HOLDERS OWNING OR HOLDING 1 PERCENT OR MORE OF TOTAL AMOUNT OF BONDS, MORTGAGES OR OTHER SECURITIES *(If there are none, so state)*

FULL NAME	COMPLETE MAILING ADDRESS
None	

HAS NOT CHANGED DURING PRECEDING 12 MONTHS / HAS CHANGED DURING PRECEDING 12 MONTHS *(If changed, publisher must submit explanation of change with this statement.)*

EXTENT AND NATURE OF CIRCULATION	AVERAGE NO. COPIES EACH ISSUE DURING PRECEDING 12 MONTHS	ACTUAL NO. COPIES OF SINGLE ISSUE PUBLISHED NEAREST TO FILING DATE
A. TOTAL NO. COPIES (Net Press Run)	500	500
B. PAID CIRCULATION — Sales through dealers and carriers, street vendors and counter sales	75	75
Mail Subscription	303	307
C. TOTAL PAID CIRCULATION (Sum of 10B1 and 10B2)	375	382
D. FREE DISTRIBUTION BY MAIL, CARRIER OR OTHER MEANS, SAMPLES, COMPLIMENTARY, AND OTHER FREE COPIES	14	15
E. TOTAL DISTRIBUTION (Sum of C and D)	389	397
F. COPIES NOT DISTRIBUTED — Office use, left over, unaccounted, spoiled after printing	111	103
Return from news agents	0	0
G. TOTAL (Sum of E, F1 and 2 — should equal net press run shown in A)	500	500

I certify that the statements made by me above are correct and complete.

SIGNATURE AND TITLE OF EDITOR, PUBLISHER, BUSINESS MANAGER, OR OWNER: *[signed]* — Editor

www.ingramcontent.com/pod-product-compliance
Lightning Source LLC
Chambersburg PA
CBHW031435040426
42444CB00006B/819